PORT OF CALL

PORT OF CALL

TALL SHIPS VISIT THE MARITIMES

ALLAN BILLARD

NIMBUS
PUBLISHING
NIMBUS.CA

Nimbus Publishing Limited
3731 Mackintosh St, Halifax, NS, B3K 5A5
(902) 455-4286 nimbus.ca

Printed and bound in Canada

NB1312

Author photo: Rick Welsford
Design: John van der Woude, JVDW Designs
Cover photo: Sherman Hines

Library and Archives Canada Cataloguing in Publication

Billard, Allan, 1949-, author
Port of call : tall ships visit the Maritimes / Allan Billard.

ISBN 978-1-77108-505-2 (softcover)

1. Sailing ships. 2. Regattas. 3. Regattas--Maritime Provinces. I. Title.

VM18.B55 2017   387.2'043   C2017-902269-5

Nimbus Publishing acknowledges the financial support for its publishing activities from the Government of Canada, the Canada Council for the Arts, and from the Province of Nova Scotia. We are pleased to work in partnership with the Province of Nova Scotia to develop and promote our creative industries for the benefit of all Nova Scotians.

I must go down to the seas again, to the lonely sea and the sky,
And all I ask is a tall ship and a star to steer her by.
—John Masefield

For Robert, my son

Table of Contents

Sails on the Horizon   **1**

Schooners, Barques, and Brigantines   **5**

The Sail Trainees   **9**

Maps   **10**

MARITIME HOSPITALITY: THE HOST PORTS   **15**

In the southern Gulf: June 30-July 2

Charlottetown **16**	Pictou **20**
Summerside **17**	Pugwash **22**
Caraquet **19**	Port Hawkesbury **24**

In the northern Gulf: July 7-9

Miramichi **26**

Preparing for the race from Halifax to France: July 29-August 1

Halifax-Dartmouth **27**

The outport program: August 4 -August 20

Sydney **30**	Shelburne **36**
St. Peter's **31**	Digby **38**
Louisbourg **33**	Annapolis Royal **40**
Lunenburg **35**	Saint John **42**

THE VESSELS

Alexander von Humboldt II 46

Atyla 48

Blue Clipper 50

Bluenose II 52

Bowdoin 56

Eagle 58

El Galeón 60

Esmeralda 63

Europa 64

Fair Jeanne 68

Geronimo 70

Gulden Leeuw 72

Impossible Dream 74

Jolie Brise 76

Katie Belle 79

Larinda 80

Lord Nelson 82

Mist of Avalon 84

Nadezhda 86

Oosterschelde 88

Oriole 90

Peter von Danzig 93

Picton Castle 96

Regina-Germania 98

Rona II 100

Roter Sand 103

St. Lawrence II 105

Sorca 106

Spaniel 109

Spirit of Bermuda 111

Spirit of South Carolina 113

Tree of Life 114

Unión 116

Vahine 118

When and If 121

Wylde Swan 122

ACKNOWLEDGEMENTS 125

Sails on the Horizon

Photo: Tom Stewart/ Maine Maritime Academy

For most of the twentieth century, the docklands of North America's cities were forgotten real estate, cluttered with crumbling wharves and vessels that no longer went to sea. What a change a generation can make.

Urban redevelopment proposals of all kinds are upping the asking prices of shoreline properties. Condos, bistros, and boardwalks are must-haves as former suburbanites seek a personal connection to the historic downtown and the sea beside it.

Long gone are the dusty warehouses and the creaking wharves lined with tar-soaked barrels. Modern harbours have restored quaysides and fully serviced berths, which complete the image of a new and well-scrubbed waterfront. And they attract tall ships.

Urban centres lucky enough to have a waterfront today find that it is a magnet for tourism.

Sail training vessels, whether Class A barques or small Bermuda-rigged ketches, are the big draw. They are the travelling minstrel shows of long ago. Wherever they go, crowds gather. Families stand in long lines to tour a restored Grand Banker, an aging clipper ship, or a replica Spanish galleon. Youngsters and even their parents dream of joining the crew and sailing off to foreign adventures.

That is why the Rendez-Vous 2017 Tall Ships Regatta has been in the planning stages for ten years. A total of thirty-six tall ships with fifteen hundred trainees on board will visit sixteen Maritime ports. Many will arrive after crossing seven thousand miles of open Atlantic, sailing in the historic wake of the great explorers. For some vessels, the event is a chance to pit their sailing skills against crews on similar vessels as they race across

Photo: Fundacion Nao Victoria

Photo: Think-Sail Inc.

the Atlantic. For others, the event is a regatta where vessels of all different rigging and classes can raise a toast to Neptune and swap sea stories. It is no surprise that Rendez-Vous 2017—a unique commemoration of coastal exploration and early settlement—will be a signature event of the 150th anniversary of Canada's Confederation.

For the Maritimes, this event reinforces an historic connection to the sea. Perhaps more importantly, though, it celebrates that successful effort to clean up harbours, breathe new life into the remaining historic structures, and encourage sustainable development where once, not that long ago, there was neglect.

This is not the first time a modern tall ship flotilla has visited Maritime shores. An initial Parade of Sail in 1984 attracted huge crowds. And again—in 1995, 2000, 2007, 2009, and 2012—Maritimers stood on every available bollard and balcony to catch a glimpse and snap a photo. The vessels reminded us of our shipbuilding traditions and reaffirmed our pride in our own tall ship icons: *Bluenose II,* HMCS *Oriole,* and *Mist of Avalon,* plus all the other ships that continue to fly the red maple leaf flag in foreign ports.

With any event like this, there is the possibility of changes in arrivals and departures. Late-breaking details are available at www.rdv2017.com.

Schooners, Barques, and Brigantines

MAGICAL AND MAJESTIC

Seen from the shore as they parade into a harbour, tall ships are majestic. They seem to glide effortlessly across the water. Up close, the dimensions of these *grande dames* become apparent.

The Class A tall ships are the ones that carry many huge square sails hung from cross spars on their masts, towering up to ten storeys above the main deck. *Bluenose II* is in this category. She and the longer gaff-rigged ships (sails which run straight up the mast with no cross spars) are also Class A tall ships because they are over 40 metres in length overall.

Class B vessels are the shorter gaff-rigged ships—the ones between 9.14 metres in length at the waterline and 40 metres in length overall.

Class C and Class D are the more modern Bermuda-rigged vessels between 9.14 metres in length at the waterline and 40 metres in length overall. Class D ships carry spinnaker sails.

Any sailing vessel, large or small, requires many hands to keep it seaworthy. That commitment can be very costly, and if there are grand voyages and ocean adventures in the plans, that means multiple crew members and more expense.

Some tall ships are operated by the military and considered valuable floating classrooms for young recruits. HMCS *Oriole* and USCG *Eagle* are active military training ships. Sail training is the best way for recruits to earn their stripes. Other vessels are owned and operated by schools and not-for-profit organizations, which rely on tuition fees and volunteer help to support their curriculum. *Bowdoin* is a floating classroom operated by the Maine Maritime Academy. The students on both these types of vessels are exposed to life skills available nowhere else but at sea.

An important part of reducing maintenance and crew costs for smaller operators is to register as a private sail training vessel and to take on-board trainees, young and old, who will learn while doing the work in return for the adventure of being at sea.

So, who is responsible for registering the ships, how does a sailing skipper find eager crew members, and what adventurous voyages can trainees take part in?

Those questions are answered by Sail Training International (STI), an umbrella association of sail training vessels, which sprang from an original organization begun in Great Britain in 1956. STI coordinates sail training tall ships all over the world through national sail training organizations. The current membership of twenty-nine countries represents 150 small and tall sail training ships.

The applicants for berths aboard sail training ships reflect the variety of social backgrounds in their home communities. Most trainees pay for their passage, but some receive subsidies if needed. Sometimes, government and commercial sponsorship is available.

STI encourages ports around the world to support its tall ship events. Ports and harbours make major contributions like no-cost or low-cost harbour facilities and important personal services like access to laundry, hot showers, and dockside entertainment for the vessel crews.

In return, the residents of the ports benefit, too. As one community official said: "This is an excellent way for families to take in some free activities, so bring your children down and enjoy the great entertainment on the waterfront." In fact, tall ship festivals and parades of sail may be the largest free outdoor festivals available anywhere. The media exposure generated for the port when the tall ships arrive is unparalleled and highly valued by communities.

SCHOONERS, BARQUES, AND BRIGANTINES

Photo: Sail Training International

The Sail Trainees

HOT SHOWERS AND GOOD MARITIME FOOD

Sail training is not actually about learning how to sail; it is more like learning by sailing.

It is an adventure for people of all ages, particularly the ones who still dream about running away to see the world. Once the ship has left port, however, there is no cellphone coverage and there is no going home. Being part of the experience means discovering the value of working as a team and becoming part of an indivisible tribe.

It is also about working very hard. Nobody ever describes a ship as a democratic institution. Trainees don't get to select their work hours, and they don't negotiate anything. They are told when to stand watch on deck, regardless of the weather, what to do, and hopefully they are told exactly how to do it. Everyone's safety depends on the trainees' ability to absorb important information and perform under pressure.

That is why the reception in the host port is critical. Being tied up alongside a jetty means hot showers and good food for the trainees. It means that there is a pub and nearby entertainment that is not on a rolling deck.

Most ports appoint liaison officers for each visiting ship, not simply to ensure friendly relations but to deliver services essential to the support and maintenance of the ships and their crews. For smaller ships arriving in a foreign port, the most frequent first question liaison officers need to be prepared for is: "Where are the showers?" After that problem is solved, the sources of supplies and services are identified.

Maps

SAILING ROUTES FOR THE TALL SHIPS

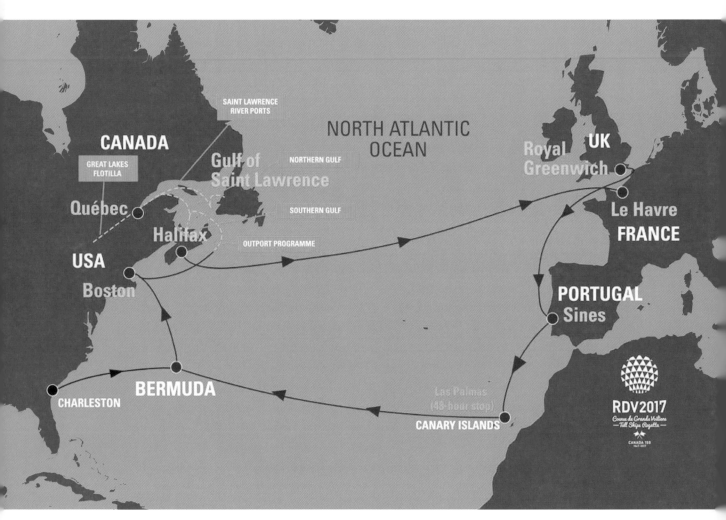

Map: Sail Training International

Ports the tall ships will visit in the Southern Gulf

Map: Sail Training International

Ports the tall ships will visit in the Northern Gulf

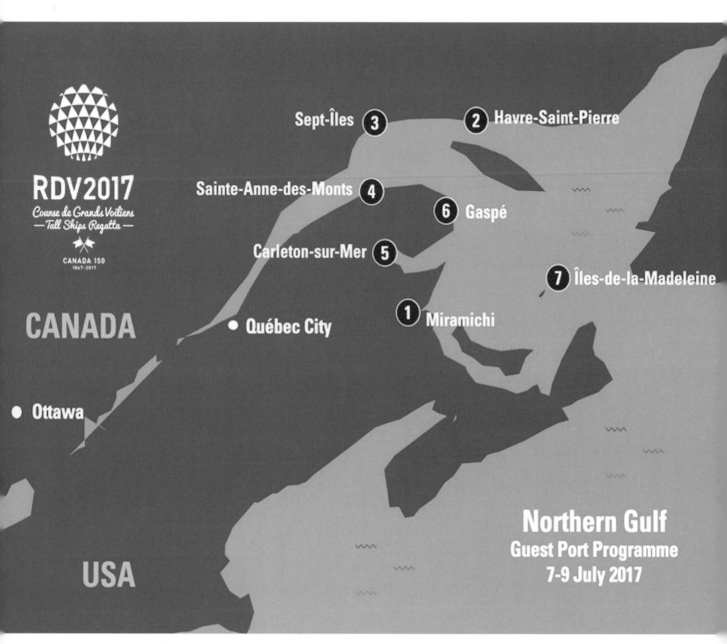

Map: Sail Training International

Ports the tall ships will visit in the Outport Programme

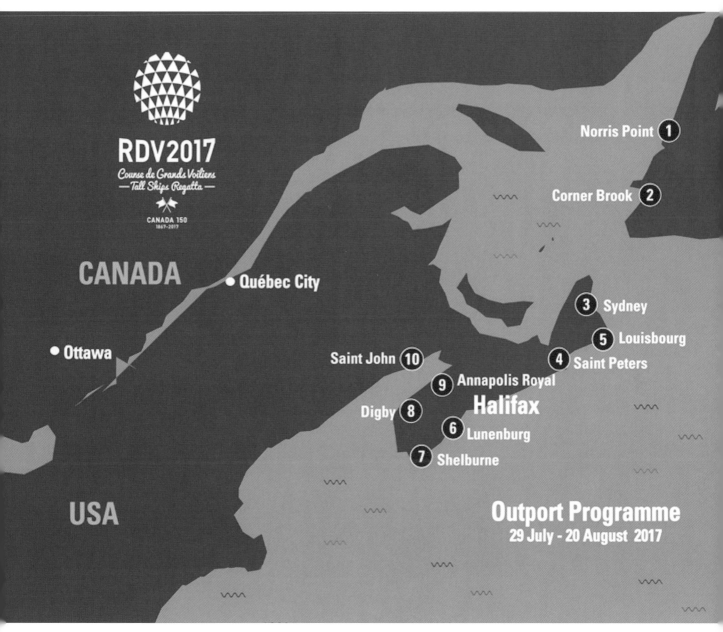

Map: Sail Training International

Photo: Sherman Hines

Maritime Hospitality

The Host Ports

IN THE SOUTHERN GULF

After eight days of high-energy racing up the coast from Boston, about seventeen vessels will get some well-deserved rest in the southern part of the Gulf of St. Lawrence. Many of the crew members will have their first experience in Canada at this point. Sailors on five Canadian-based tall ships will join them on their way to waiting ports in New Brunswick, Prince Edward Island, and Nova Scotia.

Visits like these that are the only chance the trainees have to sample the hospitality of new places and to explore the diversity of Maritime lifestyle.

As they will all discover, the Canada Day weekend is summer festival time in the Maritimes. When it is the 150th anniversary of Confederation, the excitement gets taken up another notch. Parades, fireworks, and community suppers crowd the schedule, and the visiting sailors could be excused for thinking it is all in their honour.

Charlottetown, Prince Edward Island

SOUTHERN GULF: JUNE 30–JULY 2

No city in Canada is more proud of the role its citizens played in Confederation than Charlottetown.

Back in 1864, the Prince Edward Island capital hosted the first conference to lay the groundwork for what became a new country. That was followed by a second meeting of provincial delegates later that same year in Quebec City. The bond between the two provincial capitals has been strong ever since. The third and final meetings of the Fathers of Confederation took place in London, England, in 1866 and 1867, and it is fitting that three of the visiting tall ships for Rendez-Vous 2017 come from ports near there.

With English and French-speaking Canadians, plus Dutch, Finnish, and British sailors in port, a Festival of Culture will highlight the weekend in this capital. Special appearances by local and Quebecois performers will be centre stage. There will also be Irish dancers in the city's parks, chainsaw artists, and pirate troupes.

Charlottetown, PEI
Photo: Tourism
PEI/John Sylvester

Of course, it is the tall ships that are the main attraction, and Islanders will be able to tour the vessels over the long weekend and imagine the experience the Fathers of Confederation had while sailing on similar ships some 150 years ago.

CELEBRATING CANADA DAY AT CONFEDERATION LANDING

Europa from The Hague is one of the largest and oldest tall ships in the world. She is rigged as a barque; she can carry up to thirty sails on her three masts. *Oosterschelde* is also a Class A vessel from the Netherlands but is a classic topsail schooner. Several ships from Great Britain will be in port. *Blue Clipper*, a smaller schooner, is scheduled to make an appearance. *Jolie Brise* is a cutter, very similar to a schooner but with only one mast. She is over one hundred years old and is defending her position as one of the fastest tall ships in the flotilla. Also from Great Britain, *Rona II* is a ketch sail training vessel. Like *Vahine*, a ketch from Finland, which will be in port, her sailing configuration favours these fast offshore races. Representing the US Coast Guard will be the barque *Eagle*.

Joining the tall ships will be HMCS *Charlottetown*, the modern frigate named after the birthplace of Confederation, plus the Peruvian naval barque *Union*.

After the weekend, each of these impressive vessels is off to the St. Lawrence River, making a few stops on their way to Quebec City and the major celebration there.

Summerside, Prince Edward Island

SOUTHERN GULF: JUNE 30–JULY 2

The unhurried PEI community of Summerside got its name from the agreeable summers experienced by the first European settlers. It is now well-known as the export hub for the potato industry on the Island and has also become one of Canada's most innovative users of wind power.

Four tall ships will be coming to port, showing that those modern windmills are not the only way to catch the wind. In fact, sailing vessels and lots of ocean-going traffic call upon Summerside regularly. The small city of fifteen thousand on the Northumberland Strait is just twenty-five kilometres from the Confederation Bridge and is a preferred port of call

Summerside, PEI

when sailing the Gulf waters. As a result, it has redeveloped its whole waterfront.

Within easy walking distance of the waterfront are shops and restaurants, a combined yacht and curling club, and the Island's Marine Training Institute. Not far away are the red sand beaches of the North Shore, as well as Anne of Green Gables attractions and more seafood and potatoes than any visitor could imagine.

SHARING THE SUMMERSIDE HOSPITALITY FOR THE HOLIDAY

One of the most stately Class A sailing vessels in the world will be in Summerside. *Alexander von Humboldt II* from Germany is best known for her three towering masts and unique green square sails. Also arriving from Germany, *Peter von Danzig* is a modern sloop that has used her speed to cross the Atlantic and even circumnavigate the globe for tall ship races. Another world traveller, *Picton Castle*, the three-masted barque that calls

Lunenburg, Nova Scotia, home, is arriving after a winter in the Caribbean. *Bowdoin* from Maine is rigged as a classic schooner and has been cruising the east coast and Gulf area for almost one hundred years.

When the celebrations end, these four vessels are off to the St. Lawrence River and several stops on the way to Quebec City.

Caraquet, New Brunswick

SOUTHERN GULF: JUNE 30–JULY 2

Northern New Brunswick was settled by the Acadians almost 250 years ago, partly to get far away from constant skirmishes with the British and partly to take advantage of the promise of free land. Once established on their homesteads, the Acadians found the waters of nearby Baie de Chaleur to be as bountiful as their farmland. Many of the hard-working settlers turned to fishing and made their new seaport town of Caraquet the heart of Acadia.

Ocean resources are vital to the economy of the region. Seafood exports, including lobster, crab, and shrimp, are valued at over $200 million annually. The sea drives the economy and underpins the daily fabric of the society.

One of the region's largest fleets of fishing vessels, both inshore and offshore, calls the Caraquet wharf home, as do modern fish plants and a fisheries training school. Needless to say, the arrival of five tall ships may put a real strain on the port, so several fishing vessels may move to

Caraquet, NB

temporary accommodations down the shore in Bas-Caraquet for the Canada Day weekend.

Residents and visitors from all over the Acadian Peninsula will naturally be attracted to the town's wharf to see its special arrivals. For the crews on board the sailing vessels, however, there may be a dilemma: stay and be gracious tour guides or venture into the town for a taste of Acadian seafood and hospitality.

Life in this region is not all about the sea. The Village Historique Acadien is a living museum of the daily lives of those first settlers who began farming here in 1770. Even though many remained on the land to work the farms, all Acadians agree that life would not have been the same without the tall ships that brought their forefathers here.

COMING FOR THE JULY 1 WEEKEND

The highlight of the weekend may be watching *Nadezhda*, a huge and fully rigged ship from Vladivostok in eastern Russia, sail into port. Arriving from Germany, the privately owned schooner *Regina-Germania* and her crew of six will add to the multicultural flavour. Also built in Germany but now registered in Rimouski, Quebec, the ketch *Roter Sand* with eighteen sail trainees aboard will join the fleet at the wharf. Completing the tall ship arrivals, a traditional Mahone Bay, Nova Scotia, schooner *Sorca* and her crew of eight will be in port. Plus the catamaran schooner *Impossible Dream* from Miami, Florida.

Hoping there is still room available at the town wharf, the navy's coastal defence vessel HMCS *Goose Bay* will be alongside for the weekend.

The six vessels are off to the St. Lawrence River right after Canada Day, making several stops on the way to Quebec City.

Pictou, Nova Scotia

SOUTHERN GULF: JUNE 30–JULY 2

The tall ship that brought the first settlers to Pictou, in New Scotland, was so cramped and uncomfortable that the immigrants aboard felt lucky to finally get off the *Hector* and on their deeded land grant. It didn't matter that the lands they were given to farm were thick with trees and the winters long and cold.

Pictou, NS
Photo: Darlene MacDonald/decostecentre.com

Hector was a beautiful ship, though, and a replica of that Dutch *fluyt* sits at its own quay and museum in town. It welcomes visitors aboard and offers a glimpse of what life on board a fully rigged cargo vessel, carrying 189 Scottish Highlanders, would have looked like.

The quay is also great place to catch mackerel when they are running through the harbour. To clean those mackerel, a good knife is needed. Any tall ship sailor will have a knife at hand, and in case it needs sharpening, Grohmann's factory outlet is world famous for sailors' knives. It is usually on the itinerary of crew members when they get ashore in Pictou.

What might turn out to be even more fun is the main stage at the deCoste Centre across from the wharf. It will feature traditional and multicultural performers showing the cultural mosaic that is Canada. There will also be children's activities and a welcome centre.

For some people, though, it's all about the food. Pirates will be everywhere, leading a pirate-themed scavenger hunt and encouraging visitors to take in the pancake breakfasts and local beer and lobster.

JOINING HECTOR AT THE HERITAGE QUAY

Pictou offers visitors a chance to see a striking replica of *Hector*. Having her joined by five other sailing vessels will make for an iconic Canada Day photo. Nova Scotia's *Bluenose II* will add to the occasion, as she always does, under sail or alongside. Just as impressive is *Oriole*, the Canadian Navy's sail training ketch from Esquimalt, British Columbia, and *Spaniel*, a sleek racing sloop all the way from Latvia. Perhaps overshadowing these classic smaller vessels as well as the diminutive *Hector* will be *El Galeón* from Spain and *Gulden Leeuw* from the Netherlands.

All five vessels, but not *Hector* are off to the St. Lawrence River and several stops on the way to Quebec City.

Pugwash, Nova Scotia

SOUTHERN GULF: JUNE 30–JULY 2

Pugwash is a peaceful little village on Nova Scotia's north shore. It is home to 725 souls living as their parents and grandparents have done, sharing the bountiful mineral and natural resources offered by the forests and the sea around them.

Pugwash, NS
Photo: Lisa Betts
Photography

"Growing up in the village was kind of neat," recalls Teresa Kewachuk, who teaches social studies at Pugwash District High School, "because you'd see men in suits walking down the street, going into the store, looking very happy."

She was referring to the participants at the Thinkers Lodge. Established by industrialist and native son Cyrus Eaton in 1957, his summer estate is considered the birthplace of the nuclear disarmament movement. Since the height of the Cold War, scientists from around the world regularly come together at the lodge to find a path to peace. The Pugwash Conferences were awarded the Nobel Peace Prize in 1995, a rare honour for a humble Nova Scotia village. The Nobel medal is on display at the Thinkers Lodge, a National Historic Site that sits as an inviting beacon at the mouth of the Pugwash River.

Pugwash was named "Pagwe'ak" by the First Nations, and its harbour was known for the shallow water at the estuary's mouth. Those first inhabitants recognized the advantages of the deep channel and inner harbour, however, and have welcomed many waves of settlers since the first English and Gaelic speakers arrived more than two hundred years ago.

The tall ships will be sailing in front of the Thinkers Lodge just as Pugwash is about to salute its colourful heritage on Canada Day. Residents will be combining a grand Gathering of the Clans with their annual HarbourFest. Both have been moved up to the same weekend. Having three visiting vessels available for touring will step up the program even more.

A favourite for visiting crew members will be the pancake breakfast on Saturday, followed by a parade they are invited to join. The crews, residents, and visitors will then be treated to a series of Highland Games throughout the village, musical presentations at Eaton Park, a selection of local beer and wine at the tall ships compound, as well as clams, oysters, and a lobster supper at the legion.

Spending Canada Day on the Waterfront

Katie Belle is a familiar sight in Nova Scotia where she was built. She was a favourite last year during the Pugwash HarbourFest and frequently sails the Northumberland Strait, stopping into local ports. Joining her in Pugwash this year has meant that *Atyla* of Spain will have crossed the Atlantic for the first time. Her multilingual crew will be eager to show off their vessel's classic eighteenth-century lines when she ties up next to *Geronimo*. That ultra-modern American sloop will have just completed a transatlantic crossing as part of a study term with St. George's School in Rhode Island.

The two foreign vessels are then off to the St. Lawrence River and several stops on the way to Quebec City for RDV2017.

Port Hawkesbury, Nova Scotia

SOUTHERN GULF: JUNE 30–JULY 2

Accustomed to managing large cargo ships and the extra traffic they bring, Port Hawkesbury has been a major transshipment port since the nineteenth century. Some of the largest bulk carriers on the ocean today call at the deepwater terminals, loading minerals and forest products for international markets.

Of course, smaller ships are welcomed too, and with the Canso Causeway lock just up the shore, many vessels including tall ships tie up here to enjoy the services available. On occasion, the sailors are greeted by the skirl of the pipes and an immediate march to the pub.

For this occasion, the tall ships will team up with the town for an extended Canada Day weekend celebration. A specialty of the region is the mayor's fishcake breakfast each morning until Sunday's Granville Green concert, plus a children's pirate-cove village, farmers' and artisans' market, and the five-kilometre Pirate Race. Fireworks, a parade of sail, a treasure hunt, a lobster supper, and even horse and buggy rides along the waterfront fill this elevated Canada Day weekend.

Local event hosts are encouraged that their annual Festival of the Strait will just be getting underway when the tall ships are in town.

The last time a group of sailing vessels appeared, waterfront parking was overwhelmed as residents all crowded the wharf, but organizers will be prepared this time and insist that "the more, the merrier."

Port Hawkesbury, NS
Photo: Think-Sail Inc.

IN THE STRAIT AREA FOR CANADA DAY

Spirit of South Carolina is the pride of that American state. This classic gaff-rigged schooner (like Nova Scotia's *Bluenose II*) often participates in tall ship regattas as a sailing ambassador. *When and If* is another American schooner. For almost eighty years she has been sailing the Atlantic coast of the United States and is now centred in Key West, Florida, but often escapes the Caribbean's summer heat for cool Maritime breezes. They will be joined by a third American schooner, *Tree of Life* from Rhode Island.

As the music of the Festival of the Strait starts to warm up the crowd, the three vessels will be off to small ports along the St. Lawrence River on their way to Quebec City.

Miramichi, New Brunswick

NORTHERN GULF: JULY 7–9

The Miramichi River is one of three grand rivers flowing through New Brunswick. It takes its name from *Maissimeu Assi*, meaning "Mi'kmaq Land" in the language of the local Aboriginal population. The river's major city, in turn, adopted the name when several neighbouring municipalities, including Chatham and Newcastle, were amalgamated in 1995.

Miramichi, NB
Photo: New
Brunswick Tourism

The city and its broad river have long had historic ties to the sea. The region's forests were renowned as a source for tall ship masts in the nineteenth century. Wood and paper products also supported the storied career of Max Aitken, the international newspaper tycoon who was raised there and went on to become Lord Beaverbrook. One of his lasting charitable gifts assisted with the founding of Britain's Jubilee Sailing Trust, operators of the sail training ship *Lord Nelson*, among others.

Just four years ago, tall ships visited the city, and residents enjoyed a full three days of ship tours and re-enactments from the War of 1812. This year, the five new arrivals will be offered a similar reception including a Meet the Captains Picnic and shipyard tour at historic Beaubears Island, plus dockside entertainment and a costume photo booth.

COMING UP THE BROAD MIRAMICHI RIVER

Five vessels, large and small, will sail up into Miramichi for the weekend. Three very grand Dutch tall ships, *Europa*, *Oosterschelde*, and *Gulden Leeuw* will be the tallest. HMCS *Oriole* and *Rona II* will join them before sailing off along the New Brunswick coast for the celebrations in Quebec City.

Halifax–Dartmouth, Nova Scotia

JULY 29–AUGUST 1

PREPARING FOR THE RACE FROM HALIFAX TO FRANCE

Halifax and its harbour fortifications were established as a counter to the French presence at Fortress Louisbourg and to assert British naval dominance over the Atlantic coast. It wasn't long after the city's founding in 1749 that British sailors did rule the seas. They often overwhelmed the Halifax waterfront, too.

Today, Haligonians still make a speciality of welcoming large ships of all kinds, naval and commercial. They have hosted tall ship regattas several times, starting with the initial Parade of Sail in 1984, which attracted massive crowds. Downtown office workers fortunate to have a view of the harbour stood for hours, cameras in hand, snapping photos, then requested extended lunch hours to stroll the wharves and take more photos.

To accommodate all the activity down on the harbour, Waterfront Development has helped create what organizers of Rendez-Vous 2017 call "one of the world's longest urban boardwalks." In great measure, that is an accurate way of describing the enormously popular Halifax shoreline where visiting sailing vessels, including most of the large Class A vessels, will stay.

Parks Canada and the Maritime Museum of the Atlantic are both located along the harbourfront boardwalk where they will have animated displays. There will also be special visits to Georges and McNabs Islands. Georges Island, long off limits to spectators, is a favourite backdrop for photographers as the elegant vessels file in and out of the harbour.

Local government officials, media outlets, and downtown businesses go all out for tall ships visits. Pubs fling open the doors to the crews and host special events and concerts. Parks and gardens are manicured within a leaf's breadth of pernickety perfection, and buskers line the boardwalks, enjoying the extra attention.

Across the harbour at the Dartmouth Ferry Terminal Park, the Parade of Sail will be welcomed by residents with outdoor musical presentations,

Halifax, NS
Photo: Len Wagg

the famous Pirates Landing festival hosted by Alderney Landing, buried treasure digs, as well as dockage for several of the tall ships and one of the most popular small ships, *Theodore Too*. Taste of Nova Scotia will teach children how to cook. There will be theatre performances at the Peace Pavilion, music from Symphony Nova Scotia, and daily performances on a CBC musical stage.

Playing a major role on the Rendez-Vous 2017 stage will be:

CLASS A FULLY RIGGED SHIPS

Alexander von Humboldt II
     (Germany)
Bluenose II (Canada)
Eagle (United States)
El Galeón (Spain)
Gulden Leeuw (Netherlands)
Oosterschelde (Netherlands)
St. Lawrence II (Canada)
Wylde Swan (Netherlands)

CLASS B

Atyla (Spain)
Blue Clipper (Great Britain)
Jolie Brise (Great Britain)
Katie Belle (Canada)
Larinda (Canada)
Mist of Avalon (Canada)
Sorca (Canada)
Spirit of Bermuda (Bermuda)
Spirit of South Carolina (United States)

CLASS C

Geronimo (United States)
Regina-Germania (Germany)
Spaniel (Latvia)
Tree of Life (United States)

CLASS D

Oriole (Canada)
Peter von Danzig (Germany)
Rona II (Great Britain)
Vahine (Finland)

UNCLASSIFIED

Impossible Dream (United States)

Of the twenty-six vessels scheduled to spend the weekend in Halifax, twelve will be preparing for a transatlantic crossing and the final leg of the Rendez-Vous 2017 Tall Ships Regatta, which ends with a race from Halifax to Le Havre, France.

Sail Training International, after all, is about the challenge to young sailors of racing across the open sea. The organizers have allotted four weeks for this final portion of the event. In one small way, the final leg of their journey will mirror Champlain's original trip to North America.

When the tall ships tie up in Le Havre at the same pier from which Champlain sailed, the crews will raise their glasses to the memory of those brave French sailors who first visited the New World over four hundred years ago.

Sydney, Nova Scotia

THE OUTPORT PROGRAM: AUGUST 4–6

The waterfront in Sydney, Cape Breton, was designed for events like the arrival of tall ships. Large cruise ships, private yachts, and offshore wanderers all seem drawn to the dockside and boardwalk amenities.

In recent years, the volume of traffic has increased enough to warrant a second cruise-ship berth at the port. Vessels arrive in Sydney looking for opportunities to see all that Cape Breton has to offer, including its neighbouring Cabot Trail, the Alexander Graham Bell National Historic Site, the Fortress of Louisbourg, and Bras d'Or Lake.

What they don't realize until they get there is that some of the best entertainment in the land is right there in the pavilion at dockside. Proud of their trademark fiddle music, Cape Bretoners insisted on having the world's largest fiddle, stretching sixty feet skyward, mounted on the wharf to welcome arrivals.

To honour the tall ships and Canada's 150th birthday celebration, Sydney is doing what Cape Bretoners do best: throwing a great party. The annual Waterfront Festival this year will showcase buskers, concerts, children's activities, food trucks, a teddy bear picnic, CBRM Makin' Waves Concert, mini Olympics, and fireworks.

If all that is too much for sea-bound sailors, there is also a personal crew lounge with Wi-Fi, showers, laundry, shopping, and a friendly game of soccer at Open Hearth Park.

COMING TO SYDNEY'S CRUISE SHIP PAVILION FOR THE WEEKEND

Sailing over from Corner Brook in Newfoundland, *Bowdoin* and *Lord Nelson* a special three-masted barque from Great Britain, will arrive

Sydney, NS
Photo: CBRM

to savour Cape Breton's beauty in Sydney. They will be joined by *Bluenose II*.

After their weekend in Sydney, all three will slip their lines and sail to Lunenburg. For *Bluenose II*, which recently underwent a lengthy restoration, it is a homecoming after showing off her new look in several Maritime ports.

St. Peter's, Nova Scotia

THE OUTPORT PROGRAM: AUGUST 4–6

The quaint village of St. Peter's, on Cape Breton's southern shore, has been occupied by Europeans since the sixteenth century. Even though the Portuguese, then the French, and later the English have all settled there, the name has never changed. Neither has its role as a transition from lakes to larger oceanic traffic routes. Before the canal was finally excavated, it was a haul-over road for the European fur trade, coal exports, and even smaller vessels themselves. After fifteen years of construction, in 1869 the historic

St. Peter's, NS
Photo: Len Wagg

waterway was opened and traffic could continue from the Atlantic to Bras d'Or Lake.

Still known as an important water route connecting the two bodies of water, the historic canal is primarily used by pleasure craft with less than five metres draught. Sailors wanting to enjoy the renowned cruising destinations in Bras d'Or Lake are treated to exceptional natural beauty in the recently named UNESCO Biosphere Reserve.

The sailing conditions on the lake are remarkable, but the marina in town beckons sailors to stay and enjoy the small-town hospitality. Along for the fun when the tall ships are in port, the historic town will offer three days full of pirates pirating, militia re-enactors acting, pipers piping, Mi'kmaw drummers drumming, a costume ball, and fireworks, all capped by a tall ship salute.

TYING UP AT CANAL SIDE

The picturesque and historic canal area will form a perfect backdrop for two camera-friendly schooners, *Mist of Avalon* and *When and If*. Ontario's brigantine-rigged *St. Lawrence II* with her square sails will offer a charming contrast. They will all tie up at the canal dock in St. Peter's before continuing their visits to small Nova Scotia ports and then on to Saint John, New Brunswick.

Louisbourg, Nova Scotia

THE OUTPORT PROGRAM: AUGUST 4–6

This historic town was named in honour of Louis XIV of France, and men-of-war, fishing vessels, and visitors have sailed into Louisbourg Harbour for hundreds of years. For a time, it was the largest city in North America.

Fortified against the threat of British invasion, Louisbourg was attacked twice before it was destroyed in the 1760s. The site lay untouched for many years until in the early 1960s archaeologists began to reconstruct the fortress as it was in the eighteenth century. The Fortress of Louisbourg has been called the largest reconstruction project in North America.

Louisbourg is also an historic graveyard for eighteenth-century tall ships, including what was then the flagship of the French Navy. During two major attacks by the British, ships anchored in the harbour were sunk. Of the six well-studied wrecks, some were scuttled on purpose in an attempt

Louisbourg, NS

to block the British from access to the channel into the harbour. That did not work, and several more ships were sunk. As a result, the harbour is rich in maritime artifacts.

Besides history, there are other reasons to visit Louisbourg. A major attraction is the delicious twenty-fifth annual Crabfest. On Saturday during the tall ship celebrations, local citizens will serve fresh snow-crab dinners "till they're gone." They also plan to stage musical entertainment. There will be a refreshment tent for adults and face painting and games for the young and the young at heart. Of course, families are encouraged to board the tall ships, and the crew members are invited to dig into the crab while it lasts.

COMING TO THE FORTRESS TOWN

Six vessels, large and small, will flood into Louisbourg's historic harbour. The very grand Dutch barque *Europa* and Lunenburg's *Picton Castle* will be there. *Spirit of Bermuda, Spirit of South Carolina, Wylde Swan,* and Canada's *Fair Jeanne* will join them before sailing off along the Nova Scotia coast.

Lunenburg, Nova Scotia

THE OUTPORT PROGRAM: AUGUST 10–12

Sailing into the protected harbour of Lunenburg is like a cruise back 150 years into history. Lining the waterfront are colourful sail lofts, shipyards, and fish sheds, each with their own wharf, operating much as they have been since 1867.

Settled predominantly by German and Swiss immigrants, the town was named after the Duke of Braunschweig-Lüneburg, who was the King of England, even though still a proud German nobleman. Hard-working and resourceful, the settlers built their community into the leading fishing port on the east coast and a town that UNESCO later recognized as a World Heritage Site. The precise grid of narrow streets and the heritage architecture make it distinctive and memorable.

Today, Lunenburg is home to a fascinating fisheries museum, plus the tall ships *Picton Castle* and *Bluenose II*. But even more than those treasures, the annual Folk Harbour Festival will attract thousands of people to this community for the same weekend as the tall ships are to arrive.

Many of Canada's best musical artists representing traditional and contemporary folk genres will perform throughout the town. Salt air and the sweet music will fill the waterfront, offering something for every age and musical taste, except parking. That will be impossible on the narrow streets, and shuttle buses are being arranged for spectators.

Lunenburg, NS
Photo:Len Wagg

COMING TO CANADA'S TALL SHIP TOWN

Lunenburg's flotilla of resident tall ships, including *Bluenose II*, *Picton Castle*, and the museum ship *Theresa E Connor*, will play host to visitors in August. The European-based barques *Europa* and *Lord Nelson* plus smaller ships *Fair Jeanne, Oriole, Bowdoin,* and *When and If* are to be alongside, as well as *Wylde Swan* from Holland, *Spirit of Bermuda*, and *St. Lawrence II* from Lake Ontario.

Shelburne, Nova Scotia

THE OUTPORT PROGRAM: AUGUST 14–15

For almost three hundred years, merchantmen, fishing vessels, naval frigates, privateers, rum-runners, fishing schooners, and even pirates have sailed into this deep and ice-free natural harbour. None were called "tall" ships at the time; they were simply the most efficient way to reach these shores, bringing Loyalists, newly freed slaves, and trade goods to this land of opportunity. In the spring of 1783, the harbourfront of Port Roseway teemed with over five thousand new settlers, each looking for their grant of free land and the tools to work it with.

Later the same year, the British governor decreed that the town's name should be changed to honour the then prime minister in England. His reasoning was that Lord Shelburne was in office at the time a lasting peace was achieved with America and deserved such a tribute.

By 1788, Shelburne and surrounding communities rivalled Halifax as the largest settlement on the east coast. Canada's third lighthouse, after Louisbourg and Sambro, was erected on an island in the harbour entrance, and that beacon on Cape Roseway still greets all who sail past.

As recently as two generations ago, Shelburne was just another busy Maritime port, but it is much more than that now. The downtown heritage district proudly boasts of many community gatherings and colourful festivals among the historic homes.

Residents and visitors crowd the waterfront and line the shoreline in kayaks and sailboats to celebrate their past. Even the unsettled times of pirates, privateers, and rum-runners seem to be fair game for a parade. Historical re-enactors of both the Loyalist regiments and those shady fleets of brigands play their parts together along the streets and quaysides of town.

Shelburne's Longboat Society maintains a pair of 8-metre replica longboats, which see action on the harbour waters each time there is the slightest excuse. Attired in eighteenth-century woollens, the crews row out to welcome visiting ships, promoting the town and its wooden boatbuilding history. Generations of dedication to that trade are celebrated at the Cox Historic Shipyard & Warehouse, now one of several museums that give Shelburne a frozen-in-time atmosphere enjoyed by producers of period movies.

Founders' Days kicks off the season with a re-enactors street parade in mid-July. The Nova Scotia Schooner Race Week brings several large vessels to Shelburne in early August. Songs at Sea Level brings music to the port, and the Kayak Festival draws colourful small ships to the harbour in late August.

When the tall ships arrive, they will be welcomed along Dock Street into this summer-long celebration.

VISITING OUR HISTORIC HARBOUR

Sailing into port from Louisbourg are *Europa, Fair Jeanne,* and *Spirit of South Carolina. Mist of Avalon* will be joining the flotilla, after a few days tied up at St. Peter's Canal. *Oriole* will also visit.

Each of the tall ships will continue to visit small ports in Nova Scotia and finish Rendez-Vous 2017 in Saint John, New Brunswick.

Digby, Nova Scotia

THE OUTPORT PROGRAM: AUGUST 15–16

Many Maritime communities in the 1700s were established by single boatloads of Loyalists, the British-American colonists who had opposed the revolution in the Thirteen Colonies. Often, they retained the native Mi'kmaw name for their new settlements. "Oositookun," meaning ear of land, however, didn't appeal to these New Englanders, and the Loyalists suggested honouring their leader, Admiral Digby, by naming their new town after him.

A deep and well-protected harbour, plus abundant natural resources, brought prosperity to the port. Digby grew into a shipbuilding and rail transportation hub by the nineteenth century, and even though those industries have since declined, it remains the centre for the world-famous

Digby, NS.

scallop fleet. Its commercial wharf bursts with inshore fishing vessels year-round. Nobody seems to mind that the railroad doesn't pass through here anymore.

Tourism plays a growing role in the community, as Digby's reputation for fresh seafood, particularly during the annual Scallop Days festival, can triple the town's population. It's not just during that second weekend in August. Scallop chowder, sautéed scallops, and scallops wrapped in bacon keep Water Street restaurants full all summer. Local B&Bs, inns, and resorts like the historic Digby Pines are near capacity all season, as is the pleasure-boat marina.

Several species of whales, including the enormous humpback, attract visitors. Their numbers have been steadily growing, and local guides on the whale-watching excursions guarantee sightings in the summer and fall.

Digby is a tourism destination for more than ocean life. Thousands of motorbikes crowd the harbourfront on Labour Day weekend for the annual Wharf Rat Rally.

But the hubbub on this occasion will be made by twenty-five song and dance performances in three different venues, plus wandering minstrels.

Captains and crews will be treated to special luncheons, as well as scallop-shucking displays and tastings from local wineries and breweries for the whole town. Several displays and tours will be featured around town, including a unique beehive, which will hopefully be uninhabited at the time.

ARRIVING AT THE TOWN WHARF

Mayor Ben Cleveland will welcome seven veteran vessels of sail training events to the town. And he expects the ships will attract even larger crowds than the motorcycles. *Bluenose II, Bowdoin, Lord Nelson, Picton Castle, Oriole, St. Lawrence II, When and If,* and *Wylde Swan* will join the fleet of scallopers at the town wharf. Each will have just sailed in from Lunenburg where the huge Folk Harbour Festival will have kept the crews entertained.

The annual Digby Scallop Days festival will be happening just in advance of the arrival of the tall ships. Any crew member looking for the peace of a waterfront restaurant with succulent seafood will be sure to find it just at the end of the dock.

The boats are off to an evening sailpast near Annapolis Royal then across the bay to a Festival of Sail in Saint John.

Annapolis Royal, Nova Scotia

THE OUTPORT PROGRAM: AUGUST 16

Often called the most livable small town in Canada, Annapolis Royal is one of the most historic as well.

French explorers sailed from Le Havre, sighting these shores in 1603. They recognized the beautiful and very fertile lands on both sides of the Annapolis Basin and established Port Royal, a settlement that was to become the capital of Acadia.

The arrival of these strangers and their tall ships was not lost on the native Mi'kmaw population who recorded their contact with the Europeans in several petroglyphs in what is now the nearby Kejimkujik National Park.

A dispute over the rights to the bountiful fur trade throughout the entire New World led to a long-running conflict between the French and the English. Both forces battled for over one hundred years until finally the British gained control and made Annapolis Royal the capital of their colony of Nova Scotia. The community, its river and valley, plus the surrounding countryside was named after Queen Anne, the reigning monarch.

Over the next century, the British moved to solidify their hold on Canada with an impressive shipbuilding and lumber trade in the region. Even as the timber resources dwindled and settlers began to move on to new lands in Upper Canada, the fishery still proved a dependable resource. Annapolis Royal maintained a role as a significant trading and marine transportation hub.

It is now a modern town with new businesses and a bourgeoning tourism industry. The local government has rebuilt the historic wharf to include an articulated gangway and staircase mechanism available to vessels arriving at any stage of the tide.

Channel depths in the basin are an issue for the larger tall ships, however, and navigation in the upper basin will likely be a problem for the deeper-draft vessels. That is the reason the sailpast has been scheduled for later in the afternoon when the tide will be at its highest. Following the show, a fireworks display will be set off from Annapolis Royal that will be seen in Digby and by all the ships at sea.

Annapolis Royal, NS
Photo: Dennis Jarvis

Sailing into the Annapolis Basin

Most of the tall ships, which will have rested overnight in Digby, will join a sailpast the following afternoon in the direction of Annapolis Royal: *Bowdoin, Lord Nelson, Picton Castle, St. Lawrence II,* and *Wylde Swan.* They will be joined by *Spirit of South Carolina* and *Mist of Avalon* as they come up from Shelburne to join the flotilla. *Oriole* will also visit.

Tide levels have been predicted to be fairly low just before the time of the sailpast, however, and several of the larger ships may not be able to come within camera range of the town wharf, having to turn around Goat Island in mid-basin. Those that can approach will offer a salute to Canada's most livable town, before they turn south, exit through the Digby Gut, and head to New Brunswick.

Saint John, New Brunswick

THE OUTPORT PROGRAM: AUGUST 18–20

When the tall ships arrive in Saint John, they will land at almost the exact place where shiploads of United Empire Loyalists stepped ashore in 1783. North Market Slip has been the centre of commerce for the port since that time, loading and unloading cargo shipped around the world.

The spot is also not far from where the fastest tall ship in the world was constructed. *Marco Polo,* a three-masted clipper ship, slipped down the ways at Marsh Creek in 1851 and went on to become famous for her voyages between Liverpool, England, and Melbourne, Australia—trips which took only seventy-five days!

Celebrating that historical connection between tall ships of then and now, the city has asked their festival agency, Discover Saint John, to bring together a weekend full of musical and theatrical performances. On-board tours of the large and small ships will be offered as the New Brunswick Museum and Parks Canada join in to help the most modern city on the Bay of Fundy celebrate its past.

Tying up at the new cruise ship terminals

After a late summer weekend in the port city and the end of the Canadian legs of Rendez-Vous 2017, these vessels are off on their own. *Bowdoin, Spirit of South Carolina,* and *When and If* will head back to the Atlantic seaboard of the United States. *Fair Jeanne* and *St. Lawrence II* will continue

Saint John, NB
Photo: Jillian MacKinnon/Discover Saint John

their journey on to New York City, while *Mist of Avalon* plans to return to home waters in Ontario. Barque *Europa* will head to South America while *Lord Nelson* and *Wylde Swan* will strike out back across the Atlantic. *Picton Castle* will prepare for another epic eighteen-month voyage around the world, returning to Maritime Canada in May 2019. *Oriole* is also off.

The Vessels

If it is sent by ship, then it is cargo.
If it is sent by road, then it is a shipment.

Alexander von Humboldt II

Built: 2011
Class: A
Rig: Three-masted barque
Length: 57 metres
Hull: Steel
Owner: German Sail Training Foundation
Crew: 77
Website: alex-2.eu/cms/

Crossing the Atlantic with the flotilla from Europe to Bermuda and then Boston, the new Alex will be spending Canada Day weekend in Summerside, Prince Edward Island. That visit will be followed by a cruise up the St. Lawrence River to Quebec City for the official Rendez-Vous 2017 Parade of Sail and then a return to Halifax to prepare for the race to Le Havre.

Alexander von Humboldt II was christened in 2011 as a traditional barque windjammer. That means the fore and main masts carry traditional square sails while the stern mast is gaff rigged. In all, she can carry twenty-four sails of all different shapes. Keeping it all under control are the twenty-five professional crew members who rotate through the season and up to fifty-two trainees who learn navigation and the techniques of sailing aboard a fully rigged vessel.

The history of the ship goes back much farther than six years, however. The first *Alexander von Humboldt* started her career one hundred years ago as the steel-hulled *Reserve Sonderburg*, a mobile lightship steaming from place to place around the Baltic Sea as a standby replacement for others in need of periodic refit.

At that time, it was common practice to design a large vessel along the lines of a wooden sailing ship, even though steel was quickly replacing wood, and coal-fired or diesel engines were the power sources of choice.

After sixty years of service as a lightship, plus more than a few repairs and refits, there was still some use for the solid old hull. The German Sail Training Foundation was quick to recognize her value and transformed her into a tall ship. She was rechristened as *Alexander von Humboldt*.

The new name, honouring a visionary German naturalist and explorer of the early 1800s, and a new mission as the flagship of the foundation, plus the unique green hull, served her well as she criss-crossed the world's oceans out of Bremerhaven, Germany. She remained active for a further twenty years until finally retired by the foundation. Her importance in preserving the nation's sailing traditions could not be forgotten, however, and it was decided to replace her with a new ship based upon the original lines.

The green steel hull of *Alexander von Humboldt II* and sometimes green sails are a nod to one of the original sponsors of the German Sail Training Foundation, Beck Brewery. Like *Blue Clipper* in England, *Oosterschelde* in Holland, and *Bluenose II* in Nova Scotia, as well as a Finnish brewery connected to a fully rigged ship there, a bond exists between liquor companies and vessels of the tall ship fleet. The most famous example is the sponsorship of the first tall ship races by Cutty Sark, the Scotch whiskey distiller of the same name.

Atyla

BILBOA, SPAIN

Built: 1984
Class: B
Rig: Staysail schooner
Length: 24 metres
Hull: Wood
Owner: Atyla Ship Foundation
Crew: 24
Website: www.atylaship.com

Joining the Rendez-Vous 2017 flotilla in Portugal and sailing to Boston, Atyla *will be part of the Canada Day weekend festival in Pugwash. That visit will be followed by a cruise up the St. Lawrence River to Quebec City*

for the official RDV Parade of Sail and perhaps more whale-watching. She will then return to Halifax to start the return race to Le Havre.

Atyla was handcrafted by a Spaniard who had always dreamed of sailing around the world in the wake of his nineteenth-century ancestors. When completed and launched in 1984, the schooner succeeded in recreating the image of the seafaring Spanish conquistador.

    Most of the materials for the hull were hand-carved from an African hardwood known as *iroko*. It is very difficult to work with but does not require the usual treatment with oil or varnish when used in boatbuilding. The gaff rigging is supported by masts originally made from a pair of 175-year-old Spanish pine trees, although they have now been replaced by *iroko*.

The reputation that her twenty-first-century captain and nine-member professional crew, plus the fifteen sail trainees have earned is far more collegial than the ship's nineteenth-century swashbuckling appearance. *Atyla* won the fleet's Friendship Trophy during the Black Sea Regatta a few years ago while bonding with the charismatic dolphins and porpoises there.

Often recognized for its outgoing nature, the crew is multinational; English is its working language. The crew's working mantra is teamwork and one of the few rules on board encourages them to develop relationships based upon equality. While visiting foreign ports they often seek out and support global citizenship activities.

Sail training is their stated mission, but leadership is the feature most emphasized on board. Their Watch Leader Program is geared for trainees of all ages and is being mirrored on other vessels. It recognizes initiative and personal development, and encourages candidates to take on positions of leadership.

Blue Clipper

ROYAL GREENWICH, ENGLAND

Built: 1991
Class: B
Rig: Gaff-rigged schooner
Length: 32 metres
Hull: Steel
Owner: Classic Sailing
Crew: 25
Website: www.classic-sailing.co.uk/blue-clipper

Sailing from the British port of Royal Greenwich, Blue Clipper will be a classy part of the Rendez-Vous 2017 flotilla to Portugal, Bermuda, and Boston. Her first port of call in Canada will be Charlottetown, where Islanders will share their Canada Day weekend festival with the crew. That visit will be followed by a cruise up the St. Lawrence River

to Quebec City for the official Rendez-Vous 2017 Parade of Sail, then a return to Halifax for the return race to Le Havre.

Where most sail training vessels make very efficient use of tight spaces below decks and might be called cramped, *Blue Clipper* is known as a comfortable ship. This newest member of the Maybe Sailing Fleet in Britain regularly takes part in tall ship events around Europe, the Mediterranean, and occasionally throughout the Caribbean and eastern Canada.

Built in 1991, *Blue Clipper* was once operated by the owners of Hennessy cognac to celebrate the historic clipper-ship trading routes between Europe and the Far East. Now she cruises as a sail training and charter vessel, accommodating up to twenty-four passengers in twin berth cabins with ensuites plus bunks, and has plenty of space to relax, above or below the teak deck.

Being registered as a sail training school, however, means that all those on board become active members of the crew. Led by six professional sailing instructors, crew members pitch in with hoisting and trimming sails, celestial navigation, and assisting in the galley. Even paying passengers get involved in the training and become immediately familiar with safety and emergency procedures and then the basics of a three-masted topsail schooner.

The most efficient number of masts is often debated by sailors but the decision usually comes down to the cargo carried and the expected sea conditions. In Atlantic Canada, two-masted schooners dominated the Grand Banks fishing fleet, whereas three-masted "Tern Schooners" were common among the coastal trading fleet.

Having three masts means more ropes and sails on *Blue Clipper* but adds to the speed and windward ability. In the early 1900s, some boatbuilders looking for added speed did go as high as six masts, and one very famous schooner sailed out of Boston boasting seven, but their huge size often proved unmanageable.

So, what would it cost to join the crew of this comfortable ship on its return crossing to Le Havre in August? Earlier this spring, all that luxury and adventure was advertised for £2,700, roughly $3,770 Canadian for thirty-two nights on board.

Bluenose II

LUNENBURG, NOVA SCOTIA

Built: 1963
Class: A
Rig: Gaff-rigged schooner
Length: 44 metres
Hull: Wood composite
Owner: Province of Nova Scotia
Crew: 22
Website: www.bluenose.novascotia.ca

Not a part of the transatlantic race legs of Rendez-Vous 2017, Bluenose II will spend the Canada Day weekend in Pictou. With her fresh look and a new wooden rudder, she will sail up the St. Lawrence

River to Quebec City for the official Rendez-Vous 2017 Parade of Sail, then return to Halifax, Sydney, and home to Lunenburg, with a side trip to Digby and Annapolis Royal.

Maritimers know the story of the *Bluenose* well. Renowned photographer Wallace MacAskill made her the best-loved symbol of Atlantic Canada as framed portraits graced a living room wall in most Nova Scotia homes. The rest of the country came to know her in the 1930s as the fastest Grand Banks fishing schooner and the image on the Canadian dime.

At a time when codfish was king, *Bluenose* was the champion fishing boat on the Grand Banks of Newfoundland. She regularly brought back record catches to her home port of Lunenburg, and the dorymen felt privileged to be sailing with their able skipper, Angus Walters, even if it meant harder work.

Schooners were the vessel of choice on the fishing grounds. Originally, the vessels had fore-and-aft triangular sails, but that left a lot of empty space between the masts. Skippers who wanted to carry more sail and catch

Photo: Mac Mackay

*Photo: Communications
Nova Scotia*

the light winds aloft opted for the gaff rig. That term stems from the stiff gaff spar, which secures the top side of each of the two mainsails. Raising the large four-sided sails is done with multiple ropes and tackles and often more hands are required. Extensions are added to the tops of the masts to support extra sails that fill the remaining gaps between the masts.

Her hull was also designed for racing; local naval architect William Roué made several adjustments in her lines plan to add speed. He added ballast lower on the keel to make her faster than the fishing schooners in the American fleet. He also agreed to raise the bow by half a metre, creating a larger forecastle and allowing more comfort for the crew of twenty. That added to her elegant profile and certainly did not slow her down, although some who have sailed on her point to that modification as the reason she does "corkscrew" badly.

The fishing season on the Grand Banks usually stretched from April to October. After that, the more important racing season began. Even in 1921, her first year at sea, she beat all comers and continued undefeated until the races ended in 1937. A few years after that, she was reduced to carrying freight, and *Bluenose* was lost off Haiti.

Photo: Dennis Jarvis

In 1963, Oland and Sons, a local brewery, stepped in to build a replica. *Bluenose II* was launched from the same shipyard that built the original, and she continued to sail into the hearts and living rooms of the nation.

Now freshly restored and eager to rejoin the international fleet of tall ships as Nova Scotia's sailing ambassador, she promotes the Maritime seafaring heritage and maintains a connection to the legacy of the original *Bluenose.*

Bowdoin

Built: 1921
Class: B
Rig: Gaff-rigged schooner
Length: 22 metres
Hull: Wood
Owner: Maine Marine Academy
Crew: 18
Website: mainemaritime.edu/waterfront/schooner-bowdoin/

From her home port in Maine, Bowdoin *will set out for Canada Day celebrations, fireworks, and a waterfront festival in Summerside. As part of the Rendez-Vous 2017 flotilla, she will sail with the official participants in Quebec City's tall ship parade and then travel back down the St. Lawrence to Corner Brook and Sydney. The Lunenburg Folk Harbour Festival will attract several tall ships in August, including* Bowdoin; *then it is on to Digby, Annapolis Royal, and Saint John, completing a two-month stay in Canada.*

It seems that the Maritime provinces and even the Arctic are in the bones of Maine's official sailing vessel *Bowdoin*. Since she was launched almost one hundred years ago and reinforced for ice work, this schooner has cruised northern Canada above the Arctic Circle thirty times and continues to seek opportunities to carry out scientific research there. In recognition of her significant role in the exploration of northern latitudes, she became a National Historic Landmark in the United States.

Owned by the Maine Maritime Academy since 1988 and based in Castine, she carries students on regular operations and technology cruises along the Atlantic coast. Given her age and demanding schedule, she has been overhauled several times. And then in 2015, *Bowdoin* was pulled from the water, de-masted, and given a thorough refit, including new decks.

Up to twelve students at a time sign on for the school's nautical training curriculum and can specialize in small vessel operations on their way to an

undergraduate degree in Science. In addition to the standard academic and sail training courses, students learn important details of preparing the ship for a demanding sailing season, passage planning, and the entering and clearing of foreign ports.

Sailors on other schooners in the tall ships flotilla have remarked that she carries noticeably less sail than most schooners of her size. The explanation comes from her original purpose: to sail uncharted waters in the Arctic where there is often very little wind, or sometimes far too much wind or ice to raise the sails.

Eagle

NEW LONDON, CONNECTICUT, US

Built: 1936
Class: A
Rig: Barque
Length: 81 metres
Hull: Steel
Owner: US Navy
Crew: 260
Website: www.facebook.com/CoastGuardCutterEagle

Based in New London, Connecticut, this tall ship will arrive in Charlotte-town in time to share in the celebrations of Canada Day, then continue to Quebec City, and sail back to Halifax for the Parade of Sail there.

A real favourite for spectators wherever she goes, the American Coast Guard ship *Eagle* is an elegant and fully rigged three-masted barque. Acquired from Germany after the Second World War, she immediately took on a role as a training vessel for the US Coast Guard and hosts over seven hundred cadets each year.

Recently returned from an extensive refit in a Maryland dry dock, the tall ship has had a service life extension that should allow for many more years of valuable sea time.

The vessel is operated by sixty experienced officers and crew, but it is the underclassmen from the US Coast Guard Academy who stand the

Photo: Bernard Zee

watches and handle more than two hundred lines, each cadet becoming intimately familiar with the name, operation, and function of each.

On board, the cadets and officer candidates absorb the seamanship skills and practise the navigation, engineering, and other professional theory they have previously learned in the classroom. For many, signing aboard USCGC *Eagle* is a first-time tour of sea duty and a chance to learn to serve as the leaders they will one day become in the US Coast Guard.

What spectators everywhere like most about the cadets, however, is the way they line up on the spars and shrouds when entering and leaving a port. It's the military precision that makes USCGC *Eagle* the photo magnet she is.

El Galeón

ST. AUGUSTINE, FLORIDA, US

Built: 2009
Class: A
Rig: Fully rigged ship
Length: 38 metres
Hull: Wood
Owner: Nao Victoria Foundation
Crew: 32
Website: facebook.com/elgaleonandalucia/

Now based on the Atlantic coast of North America and pleasing crowds wherever she ties up, El Galeón will be a major highlight during the Canada Day festival in Pictou. Her sail plan is to join the Rendez-Vous 2017 flotilla and visit several ports on the way to Quebec City and the celebrations of the country's 150th birthday, then back to Halifax and the huge crowds on the waterfront there.

Many tall ships are elegant; they are the beauty queens of the sea. *El Galeón* is not, however, in that category. She offers something better.

With six decks, four masts, and huge sails, Spanish galleons like this one were designed to make money for their owners, whether it was packing the holds with sailors and settlers, or transporting loads of fabulous wealth in trade goods.

El Galeón is an exact replica of a seventeenth-century merchant vessel built to carry cargo—lots of it. You can almost see the Spanish doubloons, the bolts of silk, and scattered crumbs of sea biscuits peeking out from behind the tarred coils of hemp.

It took years to research the design, ensuring that the replica was authentic to the finest detail. When she was launched in Spain in 2009, she set off to sail the waters of the world and tell of the role that galleons played in that country's West Indies colonies.

Today, *El Galeón* breathes life to the annals of explorer Ponce de León and his trade routes along the eastern shores of Florida. When she is in port, any of today's thirty-two crew members can offer visitors a guided tour through the ship and its exhibits, including historical details about three hundred years of galleon sailing technology.

The crew explains that in the historic times, each deck had a purpose, and officers were strict about keeping their sailors in their assigned places and on task.

The forecastle, pronounced fo'c'sle, is the bow of the ship. Immediately below it was the galley and quarters for some of the sailors. The bulk of the crew was accommodated down on the gun deck, though, where they could spread their mats and maintain a small amount of personal space. To their

dismay, there was never much headroom for them on the lower decks and sailors spent as little time as possible there.

Most of the daily activities, including raising the sails, were centred on the main deck where the crew, emigrant families, and even livestock spent much of their voyage. For the people there, the rest of the ship was out of bounds. Access to the hold below was through a large grille in the main deck.

The helm, where the few navigational instruments and crude charts were located, was at the stern, up on the quarterdeck. That was where the navigation officer and helmsman collaborated to catch the best winds and deliver their charges safely to port. The poop deck was named after the French word for stern and was reserved for officers who needed to maintain a broad overview of all deck levels. Only officers and perhaps high-ranking passengers had access to the stern of the vessel and the noble deck with its cabins.

Perhaps *El Galeón* is not as graceful as the schooners and barques she sails with, but she is the most authentic recreation on any of the seven seas today and a fascinating visitor to any modern seaport.

Esmeralda

VALPARAISO, CHILE

Built: 1953
Class: A
Rig: Four-masted barquentine
Length: 93 metres
Hull: Steel
Owner: Chilean Navy
Crew: 328
Website: www.esmeralda.cl

A new member of the Sail Training International flotilla, Esmeralda is scheduled to be in Halifax in June before the main participants in Rendez-Vous 2017 and visit several ports in the Northern Gulf before heading to Quebec City.

Esmeralda has a long history as a training ship with the Chilean Navy. Delivered from a shipyard in Spain to the South American country in 1954 as part of the compensation for Spanish Civil War debts, she received a huge fanfare when she arrived home in Valparaiso.

The actions of past governments in Chile have brought mixed receptions to her subsequent visits in Atlantic and Pacific ports, however. Hoping to put her service as a prison ship behind her, *Esmeralda* frequently appears in foreign countries as a floating ambassador for the new government in Chile and has become a rite of passage for officers in the modern Chilean Navy.

Originally designed as a topsail schooner, her rigging has changed over the years. Currently a barquentine, she can set twenty-one sails. Vessels with that many sails require a huge crew, and she carries over three hundred sailors, including ninety midshipmen. *Esmeralda* is not quite the tallest of tall ships, but at almost 50 metres tall, she is a most impressive sight when entering a modern harbour. The world's largest tall ship is the four-masted barque *Sedov* from Russia, at 56 metres tall!

Since her commissioning, the pride of the Chilean Navy has visited more than three hundred ports worldwide, drawing attention to her beautiful lines and the distinctive giant Andes condor figurehead, the national bird of Chile.

Europa

THE HAGUE, NETHERLANDS

Built: 1911
Class: A
Rig: Barque
Length: 45 metres
Hull: Steel
Owner: Rederij bark EUROPA
Crew: 64
Website: www.barkeuropa.com

The venerable Dutch tall ship Europa *will join the Rendez-Vous 2017 flotilla in Boston and race to the Canada Day festivities in Charlottetown and Miramichi, and several ports along the St.*

Lawrence River have requested a visit from the large square rigger on her way to Quebec City and the celebrations of the country's 150th birthday. Then she'll travel back down the river to Corner Brook, Lunenburg, and Louisbourg, then Shelburne, and finally Saint John.

Europa is over one hundred years old but continues to criss-cross the Atlantic with her crew of sixteen professional sailors and up to forty-eight sail trainees. Most winters she spends in Antarctica and often visits Pacific ports, but summers are for tall ship regattas, quite often along Canada's east coast.

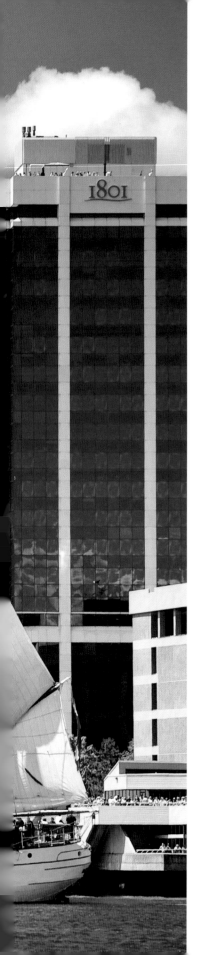

Originally built as a steel-hulled lightship, *Europa* stayed close to her station at the mouth of Germany's Elbe River for almost seventy-five years. When she was transferred to the Netherlands and refitted as a three-masted barque in 1994, her mission changed dramatically.

Now a fully rigged vessel, dedicated ocean wanderer, and registered sail training ship, she ensures that the crew is kept fully occupied with multiple tasks. No winches, but endless coils of lines and blocks with impossible names and functions face the novice sailors. Getting to know the ropes is job number one aboard *Europa*.

Easily identified by her large amount of sail, this barque became a crowd favourite when she added a full set of studding sails. They can be rigged on the outside edges of the mainsails and create an impressive figure on the horizon. She can hoist a total of thirty sails and do more than twelve knots when the wind is favourable, running on canvas and co-operation the Dutch way: with quiet teamwork.

English is the working language on board and the crew encourages the trainees to be a part of everything— climbing the rigging, assisting in the galley, and taking a watch at the helm during the day and the night, in wind, rain, and sunshine.

Aside from the sailcloth that hangs from the spars, another complete set is stored in the forepeak. Not just emergency replacements after storm damage, the extra sails are completely changed out when *Europa* enters the Southern Ocean. There, the winds can be fierce, and stronger materials are needed.

Back in the tropics the older ones are reinstalled. In the doldrums with low wind, the sails chafe on the rigging or get sun bleached and weakened. The compromised sheets are used until the vessel leaves the gentle breezes of the Caribbean, then taken down and repaired before being stored for another trip.

Fair Jeanne

Built: 1982
Class: A
Rig: Brigantine
Length: 34 metres
Hull: Wood
Owner: Bytown Brigantine Inc.
Crew: 40
Website: tallshipsadventure.org/our-fleet/

From her home port on the St. Lawrence River, Fair Jeanne's *participation in the Rendez-Vous 2017 flotilla will begin with the official Parade of Sail in Quebec City. Corner Brook, Newfoundland, will receive a rare tall ship experience in late July, including* Fair Jeanne, *then it is on to Louisbourg and Shelburne. She will add New Brunswick to her port visits, with a final weekend in Saint John.*

Fair Jeanne is the 1982 creation of Captain Thomas Fuller. After retiring from the Canadian Navy, he built the 36-metre brigantine in his backyard just outside of Ottawa and sailed with his wife, Jeanne, all over the Caribbean and western Europe. Since then, it has been a windjamming adventure school for over two thousand teenage trainees.

This vessel, one other brigantine, and two support vessels are operated by the Bytown Brigantine Academy. For the lucky youth who get to learn while living like sailors, summer school credits are awarded by the Ontario Ministry of Education.

A permanent crew of thirteen leads the adventures for up to twenty-seven youth at a time. Even the captain, who was himself once a sail trainee on board, participates in the effort to challenge the youth both physically and mentally. Safety on board is the first topic covered by the instructors, and once that is covered, trainees quickly learn the rest.

It is more than just handling the sails. There is also standing watch at the helm, handling all the lines, weather forecasting, navigation, radio operations, and of course, ship maintenance.

Photo: Sail Training
International

They also master the differences between tall ships. There are several classes, generally defined by the number of masts they have and the way their sails are rigged. *Fair Jeanne*, a brigantine, has two masts; the front one has a cross spar, or yard, and can carry square sails, while the other carries fore-and-aft sails. There can also be one or more jibs up front on most sailing ships, regardless of their rigging.

Like over fifty other sail training tall ships, *Fair Jeanne* is a registered member of the international Blue Flag Scheme. The flag it flies shows everyone that they have pledged to protect all harbour waters while in port as well as the seas they sail on.

Geronimo

Built: 1998
Class: C
Rig: Cutter
Length: 21 metres
Hull: Fibreglass
Owner: St. George's School
Crew: 12
Website: www.stgeorges.edu

Based in New England, Geronimo *will join the Rendez-Vous 2017 flotilla in Boston and race to the Canada Day festivities at dockside in Pugwash, then to Quebec City for more celebrations of the country's 150th birthday with the Parade of Sail. Her return to Nova Scotia and the Halifax waterfront will be the final leg of her Canadian voyage for the year.*

Geronimo is an ultra-modern 21-metre sloop, built twenty years ago in Rhode Island. She is not very long but is one of those vessels that looks like she is going very fast, even when still standing at the wharf.

Operating out of St. George's School in Newport, Rhode Island, her cruises introduce high school students to a variety of marine sciences and sailing skills. The sleek tall ship, with three to four professional sailors and seven to eight young trainees, has taken on many open ocean voyages and regularly sails south from New England to the Caribbean and northward for the Maritime provinces. Last winter she completed her longest voyage yet, over three thousand nautical miles across the Atlantic Ocean from the Canary Islands. Each adventure is followed by a toast to *Geronimo* and maybe Poseidon.

Students are attracted to the hard work and multi-dimensional training on *Geronimo.* They must keep up with the teamwork required on board a tall ship while maintaining a good academic standing and managing a full course load.

1277

The skills and lessons offered are vastly different from landlocked schools, particularly the fieldwork of gathering data for the Center for Sea Turtle Research at the University of Florida. Teams of students collect, tag, and release the animals while gathering information on migration patterns.

All that makes for busy days and nights, but their reward comes from places they visit, such as the Azores, Canary Islands, Puerto Rico, and Pugwash.

Gulden Leeuw

KAMPEN, NETHERLANDS

Built: 1937
Class: A
Rig: Topsail schooner
Length: 55 metres
Hull: Steel
Owner: Class Afloat –West Island College
Crew: 84
Website: sailonboard.com/vessel/gulden-leeuw/

Over eighty years old and still plying the world's oceans, Gulden Leeuw *will be a crowd favourite in Bermuda and Boston as part of the transatlantic fleet. In Canada, her first port of call will be Pictou on Canada Day. Then she will travel on to Miramichi and Quebec City to celebrate the country's 150th birthday with the Parade of Sail and Rendez-Vous 2017. On her return to Nova Scotia and the Halifax waterfront, preparations will be made for the final ocean crossing to Le Havre, France.*

Starting life as a robust and ice-strengthened support ship in 1937, *Gulden Leeuw* was originally called *Dana*. After seventy years at sea, her greatest remaining asset was her good bones, so she was chosen for transformation into a three-masted topsail schooner. Rechristened and launched again in 2010, she immediately opened her enormous deck to sail trainees.

The sail plan of a topsail schooner makes the vessel manoeuverable and efficient in both heavy and light winds. It includes two or three large

square sails atop the foremast, and two other masts with huge gaff-rigged sails, as well as optional sails. All that puts an enormous strain on the keel, particularly at top cruising speeds. Had she not been constructed to handle the heavy sea conditions of the North Atlantic, *Gulden Leeuw* could never have accepted the stresses from the rigging.

Her redesigned lower decks are home to a crew of sixty sail trainees under the direction of twenty-four professionals. Nine months of the year *Gulden Leeuw* offers senior high school and university programs to approximately twenty ports while sailing to four continents.

Her owner has made every effort to make her comfortable, as well as sturdy and multi-purposed. The ship has a flair of 1930s luxury and has found a marketing niche for corporate hospitality, seminars, and day trips. Passengers seem drawn to the after-deck where the atmosphere of the Captain's VIP Lounge brings to mind tales of adventure and intrigue.

Impossible Dream

MIAMI, FLORIDA, US

Built: 2002
Class: UNCLASSFIED
Rig: Bermuda-rigged catamaran cutter
Length: 18 metres
Hull: Carbon fibre
Owner: Shake-A-Leg Miami (SALM)
Crew: 8
Website: www.impossibledream.us

When a tetraplegic yachtsman has a dream to sail the Atlantic, the vessel he requires must be unique. So it was with the innovative catamaran schooner Impossible Dream.

Launched near the British port of Plymouth in 2002, she was the first sailing boat that could be controlled by a palmtop computer, thus making it possible for just one person, in a wheelchair, to fulfill his dream.

After a dozen years of sailing with her push-button technology, and after introducing hundreds of other disabled sailing enthusiasts to the possibilities of an independent life at sea, *Impossible Dream* was transferred to new owners in Miami, Florida.

As part of a charity headquartered in Coconut Grove in southern Florida, the Shake-A-Leg Miami Community Watersports Center has become a public/private partnership with the city of Miami and a host of community-based organizations. It invites people with disabilities, disadvantaged children and their families, wounded soldiers, as well as the community at large, to take on new challenges.

Photo: Harry Horgan/
Courtesy of Shake-A-
Leg Miami

For the past three years, her professional skipper and crew have encouraged people to take up the joy of sailing. To facilitate that, ramps and wide passageways circle the main deck and serve the crew and guests, making mobility a non-issue. Like *Lord Nelson*, the British barque featured in this book, *Impossible Dream* has an elevator to access the cabins below. The unique design is more than purposeful. The owners hope that it will show how beauty and functionality can coexist.

The tall ship journey for *Impossible Dream* starts in Bermuda where she joins the international fleet for the race to Boston and then up to Caraquet, New Brunswick, for Canada Day weekend. After several stops along the St. Lawrence River and in Quebec City, she will return to Halifax and the tall ships' challenge before returning home to Miami.

Jolie Brise

HAMBLE, ENGLAND

Built: 1913
Class: B
Rig: Gaff-rigged cutter
Length: 17 metres
Hull: Wood
Owner: Dauntsey's School Sailing Club
Crew: 12
Website: www.joliebrise.com

Departing from the British port of Royal Greenwich, Jolie Brise will try to lead the flotilla to Portugal, Bermuda, and Boston. Her first port of call in Canada will be Charlottetown where Islanders can share the Canada Day weekend festival with her crew. That visit will be followed by a cruise up the St. Lawrence River to Quebec City for the official Rendez-Vous 2017 Parade of Sail, then a return to Halifax for the race to Le Havre.

Jolie Brise is fast. Fashioned from solid oak with steel and lead in her keel, she has become one of the most famous tall ships in the world. That status comes not just because she is still very active on the tall ship circuit after

one hundred years, but because this British cutter still wins her class in ocean races and often wins overall. Her competition results are likely due to her small size and huge sail area, but still it is surprising that a sail training vessel so old can perform so well. Thus, her fame.

Originally built in Le Havre, France, she served at the tail end of the Age of Sail when harbour pilots needed to be quickly ferried out to incoming clipper ships. Even in today's age of giant container ships, harbour pilots still need to be delivered to waiting ships, but they have their own harbour craft on standby. The few remaining classic cutters are now available as sail training vessels.

With the short hull length and the ability to raise sails both fore and aft, cutters were designed to take quick advantage of changes in wind direction. Either running with or against the breeze, they were highly manoeuverable. In fact, they were so successful in their role, that even today, most small motorized harbour craft are often called cutters.

With all that sail area on *Jolie Brise* and no winches, the captain, mate, and ten young trainees must work extremely hard. Co-operating as an efficient team is the overriding principle of the Dauntsey's School Sailing Club, which has owned her for the past forty years. Sailors are involved in all aspects of her maintenance and operation from navigation, standing watches and setting and trimming sails to cooking and cleaning. All that, and a chance to skim across the open Atlantic, brings the trainees back for more.

As self-described wind seekers, crew members on *Jolie Brise* this year hope to challenge the Atlantic and win yet another overall tall ships race. They also signed on to have a chance to see narwhals and humpbacks when in Canada. With their luck and attention to the sea conditions, that could happen.

Nota bene: The *Jolly Breeze,* located in New Brunswick, was finely crafted in New Zealand in 1989 as a private, ocean-sailing yacht with fine woodwork, gleaming bronze, and flowing lines. She has since sailed around the world and is now operated as a local sightseeing vessel in Saint Andrews, New Brunswick.

Katie Belle

STEWIACKE, NOVA SCOTIA

Built: 2015
Class: B
Rig: Gaff-rigged cutter
Length: 24 metres
Hull: Wood
Owner: Private
Crew: 8
Website: www.facebook.com/CameronShipyardsLtd

Sailing into Pugwash will be like going home for the crew of Katie Belle. While not yet a world traveller or a frequent participant in tall ship events, she is fast becoming a welcome sight in Halifax and along Maritime shores.

During the Age of Sail, even the smallest Maritime ports were busy with lumber mills and shipyards. Looked at today, these places seem far from navigable waters. But communities like Stewiacke, some thirty-five

Photo: Waterfront Development

kilometres up river from the Bay of Fundy, once rang out with the sounds of the adze and caulking mallet.

That was the heritage that sparked a six-year dream in the hearts of two young cousins there. During their childhood, Evan and Nick Densmore heard the stories of traditional Nova Scotia shipyards and decided to build their own gaff-rigged schooner. Carefully following the plans approved by their grandfather and honouring the traditions of practiced shipwrights, the two craftsmen were joined by many local residents who volunteered to be a part of the project.

Katie Belle was the first of her kind to be launched on the Stewiacke River in living memory, and it took timing to catch the incoming tide at its peak. As she floated away from the wharf, her young builders christened their schooner in honour of the family, which founded the original Cameron Shipyards in nearby Maitland several generations before.

From Stewiacke to Pugwash and then down to South Carolina, the vessel received careful attention while the final rigging and sea trials were completed. Now touring the coast of the three Maritime provinces, the two cousins bring their own dream and their family's history back to life.

Larinda

BRIDGEWATER, NOVA SCOTIA

Built: 1996
Class: B
Rig: Staysail schooner
Length: 18 metres
Hull: Reinforced concrete hull
Owner: Larinda's Landing
Crew: 6
Website: www.larindaslanding.com

After many years of toil, the American builders of Larinda *launched their dream boat in 1996.* Larinda *took the lines of a 1767 Boston schooner and was fitted with a 1928 diesel engine, one of only two left in the world.*

Photo:Dennis Jarvis

She immediately sailed off to visit eight foreign countries and took part in several tall ship festivals. The replica schooner, with her unique engine and the rigging of a Chinese junk, became, for a while, the permanent home of her builder and his wife.

Larinda was only seven years old when she sat at a Halifax pier in September 2003. A hurricane had been forecast and the owners had chosen to await favourable winds for their return to Cape Cod. It turned out to be a night of horrors as they barely saved themselves while watching their home sink at the wharf. If recreating a historic schooner is a dream, restoring a sunken one can be a nightmare. Decontamination and repairs proved too costly for the owners who sold her to Nova Scotia operators.

Now part of a new vision, *Larinda* has become a welcome sight around Eastern Canada. Her bright work regularly polished, the hardwood trimming well cared for, and that classic frog figurehead all make for a special photograph for fans of sailing vessels. Maritimers all remember the September night when Hurricane Juan struck Halifax. The sad story of *Larinda*'s sinking and the positive outcome are part of that memory.

Sailing up from her berth in Bridgewater, Nova Scotia, *Larinda* is expected to visit several local ports along with the foreign vessels. Best known on the Halifax-Dartmouth waterfront, she is sure to draw huge crowds at Alderney Landing.

Lord Nelson

SOUTHAMPTON, ENGLAND

Built: 1985
Class: A
Rig: Three-masted barque
Length: 40 metres
Hull: Steel
Owner: Jubilee Sailing Trust
Crew: 50
Website: classic-sailing.co.uk/vessels/tall-ship-lord-nelson

From the historic tall ship port of Southampton, Lord Nelson *will take the northern route, by Iceland, to join the fireworks and celebration of Canada's 150th birthday as part of the Rendez-Vous 2017 flotilla in Quebec City. Then she'll travel back down the river to Corner Brook, Newfoundland, and Sydney. The Lunenburg Folk Harbour Festival will attract nine tall ships in August, including* Lord Nelson. *Then she is on to Digby, an evening sailpast in Annapolis Royal, and a weekend in Saint John.*

Tall ships that circle the globe with forty young sail trainees are not that
uncommon. What *Lord Nelson* does, however, has made her a pioneer.
Where others are crowded, with precious little space for amenities, this
fully rigged vessel has wide companionways, spacious cabins, shower seats,
and adjustable basins. There is even an elevator.

Lord Nelson was two years in the making. The Jubilee Sailing Trust,
a charitable foundation in Britain, which was set up in part by New
Brunswick native Max Aitken, wanted to enable people with disabilities to
sail and that, it was felt, could be best achieved with a purpose-built and
uniquely equipped vessel.

Designed and built to accommodate wheelchairs, she is also fitted with alerts geared to hearing-impaired sailors, plus Braille markings and a speaking compass to address a variety of skill levels at sea. People of all abilities work side by side aboard this three-masted barque, on equal terms. The same was true even in the shipyard back in 1986 when many apprentices were involved in her construction.

Stressing inclusiveness in the day-to-day running of the ship, the captain and nine professional crew members encourage trainees of all abilities to take the helm, climb the masts, set the sails, and learn navigation skills. Not shy about their mandate, the crews often sail up the Thames River, brandishing their abilities. These leadership skills mirror the legend of their famous admiral namesake who overcame physical challenges himself, and are recognized by the Duke of Edinburgh Awards as well as Rotary International, which subsidizes trainees.

The Jubilee Sailing Trust has been so pleased with the *Lord Nelson*'s "All Abilities, All Aboard" operation and performance that they subsequently ordered a second, larger barque, *Tenacious*. Sailing more in the southern hemisphere, she regularly visits Australia, New Zealand, the Falkland Islands, and South Africa. To date, the two vessels have made space for over forty thousand trainees.

Mist of Avalon

IVY LEA, ONTARIO

Built: 1967
Class: B
Rig: Gaff-rigged schooner
Length: 22 metres
Hull: Wood
Owner: Liverpool Bay Packet Co. Ltd.
Crew: 11
Website: www.mistofavalon.org

Following her participation in the 150th celebrations in Quebec City, Mist of Avalon will sail down the St. Lawrence River to Cape Breton and St. Peter's Canal. She and her crew will visit two other ports in her native

Photo: Rob Stimpson

province, Halifax and Shelburne, plus an evening sailpast in Annapolis Royal, then spend the final weekend of Rendez-Vous 2017 in Saint John.

Mist of Avalon sails from her home port in Ontario, but she is an original Grand Banks gaff schooner, built in Mahone Bay, Nova Scotia, in 1967. Designed as a schooner but destined to be a motor vessel, she was named the *Liverpool Bay* and was active with the Nova Scotia fishing fleet for twenty years. The fortunes of that industry changed, and she was overhauled in 1992, transferred to Ontario, and reborn as the elegant namesake of Avalon, a mythical island of rebirth.

When seen from a distance, she does seem to be emerging from the mists of a long-forgotten time. Avalon was the fabled resting place of King

Arthur and although several islands on the southwest coast of England claim to be the setting for those myths, it does seem that fog-bound coasts and sailing vessels did play major roles in those Anglo-Saxon times.

As a schooner-rigged vessel, she carries her sails fore-and-aft. When all are fully set, she has that classic schooner profile so well known in the Maritimes. The two four-cornered gaff sails are the main sources of her speed and steerage, and there are four others she can raise when the wind is right. The highest, which can be set above the mainsails, are the gaff topsails, which are set over nineteen metres above the deck.

Very much a working vessel, she is a frequent participant in tall ship events as well as having carried hundreds of sail trainees, starred in feature films, and worked the corporate scene as a floating ambassador in festivals and boat shows. Wherever she makes port, she is a popular attraction for admirers who are full of questions about life on the high seas.

Below decks, accommodations for the crew of eleven are typical of a working boat: well-appointed but compact. A wood-burning stove adds charm to the salon area, as well as the heat needed on misty evenings anchored off a Celtic isle.

Nadezhda

VLADIVOSTOK, RUSSIA

Built: 1990
Class: A
Rig: Fully rigged ship
Length: 95 metres
Hull: Steel
Owner: Far Eastern State Maritime Academy
Crew: 191
Website: msun.ru/en/fleet_en_nadezhda

Photo:
Sailonboard.com

Nadezhda *will sail to Royal Greenwich in England and the official start of Rendez-Vous 2017, including the race to Portugal, Bermuda, and Boston. The huge vessel will enjoy the Canada Day festivities in Caraquet and be a part of Rendez-Vous 2017 in Quebec City before returning to Europe.*

This huge sail trainer is based in Vladivostok on the Pacific coast of Russia and rarely visits the eastern seaboard of North America. *Nadezhda,* sometimes called Nadia for short, is translated as *Hope*. She is strikingly similar to five older fully-rigged Russian ships. *Mir* (translated as *Peace*), has visited Canada on several occasions, along with *Dar Mlodziezy* (*Gift of Youth*), *Khersones, Pallada,* and *Druzhba.* To distinguish them from each other at sea, they have been decorated in different colours.

Ships of this class are as long as a Canadian football field and when the winds are right, *Nadezhda's* crew of fifty-one, plus one hundred and forty trainees, all pitch in to manually raise fourteen large square sails and twelve fore-and-aft sails. It's a big operation!

Since 1992, the three-masted frigate *Nadezhda* has been dedicated to the education of new generations of Russian seamen under the direction of the Maritime State University in Vladivostok. It has been a little known but important port for the nation on the Pacific coast, and the government wants to bring it to the attention of the world.

She started on that mission in 2002 with a visit to Korea for the FIFA World Cup and then in 2003 by circumnavigating the globe, visiting thirty ports in twenty countries. She went on to represent the Russian Federation in 2009, at the 600th anniversary of the port Shendzhamen (Peoples' Republic of China), one of the oldest ports in the world. All that while putting more than two thousand cadets through their classes in sail training and ocean environmental monitoring.

Oosterschelde

ROTTERDAM, NETHERLANDS

Built: 1918
Class: A
Rig: Topsail schooner
Length: 40 metres
Hull: Steel
Owner: Shipping Company Oosterschelde
Crew: 31
Website: www.oosterschelde.nl/en

Returning from the Antarctic, Oosterschelde *will join the Rendez-Vous 2017 event in Bermuda for the race back to Boston and then head straight to Charlottetown for Canada Day on Confederation Quay. After some well-earned downtime for her crew, the vessel goes to Miramichi and Quebec City for the main Rendez-Vous 2017 event and back to Halifax to prepare for the return leg of the race to Europe.*

The name *Oosterschelde* refers to the eastern branch of the Schelde River, a very important commercial waterway flowing through three European countries.

Built in 1918, the ship carries the river's name and is the last of a large fleet of freighters that sailed under the Dutch flag. Hundreds of tons of trade goods were collected from ports all over the world. Bricks, fish, and bananas filled her holds before she traded hands several times then finally retired.

In 1992, after a complete transformation and a royal relaunching ceremony, she returned to the sea, this time prepared to take trainees and passengers aboard and to share her tales of ocean adventure.

When in port she regularly hosts corporate presentations, receptions, and parties of visitors eager to learn about the Age of Sail. She is rarely home in Rotterdam, however, before another ocean voyage calls her to sea.

Registered as a national historic monument in the Netherlands, this topsail schooner is a favourite wherever she sails. A well-seasoned world traveller, with a crew that enjoys the huge crowds she attracts, *Oosterschelde* presents herself as a *grande dame* of the sea.

She has opened her decks to young and old, as well as to groups with special coaching needs. On the water, passengers and crew are rarely idle as everybody on board is expected to learn how to trim the sails, navigate, take the helm, participate during watches, and share in the routine of shipboard maintenance.

It doesn't take long for new recruits to get into the rhythm of a blue water passage. It is partly the hard work but perhaps more likely the sheer beauty of the Atlantic. The sea has an effect on people. It empowers them, but one thing is optional: climbing the masts is a necessary part of operating a square rigger, but stowing the sails atop the three masts is not for everybody.

Oriole

CFB ESQUIMALT, BRITISH COLUMBIA

Built: 1921
Class: D
Rig: Marconi-rigged ketch
Length: 31 metres
Hull: Wood
Owner: Royal Canadian Navy
Crew: 21
Website: www.readyayeready.com

In her role as the sail trainer for the Royal Canadian Navy, HMCS Oriole will give her young recruits an open ocean experience with the tall ship race from Bermuda to Boston and then into the Gulf of St. Lawrence and Canada Day in Pictou. Their journey will take them to

*Charlottetown, along the coast of New Brunswick to Miramichi and
then up the St. Lawrence River to Québec City for the Parade of Sail.
She had added ports to her planned visit and now has stops in Halifax,
Lunenburg, Shelburne, Digby, Annapolis Royal, and Saint John.*

This 30-metre sailing ketch is celebrated as the oldest and longest-serving
vessel in the Royal Canadian Navy. Built in Toronto in 1921, she was privately
owned until leased to the RCN as a training vessel during the Second World
War. In 1952, after hundreds of young sailors were trained in seamanship,

*HMCS Oriole
Photo: A.Davey/
flickr.com*

Oriole was given a thorough refit, and the navy officially commissioned her into the fleet based in Halifax. Two years later she was transferred to the west coast and still serves at the Officer Training Centre there.

At one point on the voyage from Halifax around to the Pacific, she was met by a second Canadian naval vessel. During the customary exchanges of protocol, the crew of *Oriole* was amazed to discover that most other naval vessels seemed to have showers, hot water, storage space, separate bunks, and a radio that connected them with headquarters. The decks of their cramped ketch leaked and water would often drip into their morning porridge while they listened to messages from Singapore, although they could raise nothing from home.

After arriving at the naval base in Esquimalt, British Columbia, significant upgrades were made to her generator, hull, radio, and other systems. *Oriole* was then completely prepared to deliver the training that the navy recruits needed. Today, she still trains naval recruits and hosts five-day Youth Adventure Challenge tours designed to build confidence and encourage teamwork.

Crew aboard the vessel proudly show the logbook in which Pierre Trudeau recorded his visit and wonder if, as the new prime minister, his son might return. In the meantime, they host continual visits of sea cadets and ongoing protocol exchanges.

Peter von Danzig

KIEL, GERMANY

Built: 1992
Class: D
Rig: Bermuda-rigged sloop
Length: 17 metres
Hull: Fibreglass
Owner: Akademische Segler-Verein in Kiel
Crew: 12
Website: www.asv-kiel.de

Beginning the race at the official start point in Royal Greenwich, Peter von Danzig *will stay with the event all the way to Summerside and*

Photo: Wolfgang Barnitzke/ Marinetraffic.

Canada Day at the dock there. The German sloop will be a part of Rendez-Vous 2017 in Quebec City and then return to Nova Scotia and the Halifax waterfront to prepare for the race back to Le Havre.

The first vessel of several vessels called *Peter von Danzig* goes back before the time of Columbus. It was built in France, and while delivering a very valuable cargo of salt to Poland, was struck by lightning and abandoned in Danzig (present-day Gdansk). When hostilities arose between emerging European nations, an enterprising privateer made it seaworthy enough to hunt down English merchantmen who dared enter the Baltic until that war ended.

There have been a few other Peters since, but this latest edition of *Peter von Danzig* is a German ocean-racing sloop based in Kiel. That is not that far from the historical Polish port of Danzig, but this vessel sails as a sea school rather than a swashbuckler.

Owned and operated by the Akademischer Segler Verein in Kiel (ASV), a student-run sailing club affiliated with Kiel University, the 17-metre sloop has been optimized for blue water cruising. *PVD,* as the vessel is known in the fleet, has raced across the Atlantic several times, to the absolute thrill of the trainees aboard. Trimming and swapping out different sails on deck provides the life lessons that no shore-based classroom could have offered them.

Down below are accommodations with single berths, a cozy salon and common area, plus all the sailing technology required for offshore cruising.

Picton Castle

Built: 1928

Class: A

Rig: Three-masted barque

Length: 45 metres

Hull: Steel

Owner: Barque Picton Castle

Crew: 52

Website: www.picton-castle.com

Returning from another of her world cruises, Picton Castle *will join the Rendez-Vous 2017 event in Bermuda for the race back to Boston and then head straight to Summerside for the Canada Day party there. After some well-deserved down time for the tribe on board, the vessel goes to Québec City for the main Rendez-Vous 2017 event and back to Newfoundland and Cape Breton before finally returning to Louisbourg and home to Lunenburg for the Folk Festival weekend. Then the crew goes back to sea for a port visit in Digby, an evening sailpast in Annapolis Royal and a final weekend in Saint John, all the while planning the next adventure.*

Since 1997, this ship has sailed around the world six times and made many voyages to exotic ports which most people thought only existed in dreams. All the while her skipper and crew have introduced over one thousand people, young and old, to a daily routine of a traditional square-rigger. Such is the day-to-day life of *Picton Castle.*

Originally an English fishing trawler hard at work on the North Sea, in the Second World War she became a minesweeper and convoy escort, then languished at forgotten wharves. When looking for a vessel he could fit out as a full square-rigged sailing ship, Captain Daniel Moreland found *Picton Castle* in Norway and brought her to Lunenburg where skilled tradespeople transformed her into a seaworthy square-rigger.

Everyone on board this barque works, not just at learning the traditional jobs of sailing a tall ship, but they join in hauling on lines, mending sails,

helping in the galley, going aloft, keeping lookout, and scrubbing the oiled pine decks. It is hard work, but nobody promised them that it would be easy.

She can carry up to fifty-two crew members but they have limited personal space, in upper or lower bunks. The main saloon, with its rich mahogany tables is their bedroom, dining room, living room, and classroom. Many of the crew are housed there, as well as in the forepeak, in the after cabin, and even in the fo'c'sle. In fair weather, most meals are eaten on deck. That is where the galley is, on deck and sheltered only partially from the wind. Its 1893 cookstove is like the original one supplied to the vessel one hundred years ago, but it no longer burns coal.

Of course, all this hard work and the sparse living conditions are part of a ship that sails into foreign ports like Vanuatu, Galapagos, and Bali so there are compensating advantages to sailing on *Picton Castle*.

By the way, there really is a Picton castle. It is a medieval structure built in Wales by a Flemish knight that dates back to the late 1200s. Still today, it is inhabited by his descendants.

Regina-Germania

FRANKFURT/MAIN, GERMANY

Built: 1984
Class: C
Rig: Gaff-rigged schooner
Length: 14 metres
Hull: Steel
Owner: Uwe Herrmann
Crew: 6–8
Website: www.regina-germania.de

Having spent the past winter in the Caribbean, the tall ship race from Bermuda to Boston will be the first leg of the event for German Regina-Germania. She will sail straight from there to Caraquet for Canada Day festivities and then on to Quebec City with the balance of the Rendez-Vous 2017 flotilla. The quick trip to Canada will include final preparations in Halifax for the race back home to Europe.

There is always more than one way to rig a sailboat. Some have large gaff-rigs, like the schooner *Bluenose II*; others have tall triangular sails as on the ketch HMCS *Oriole*, called a Bermuda rig. There are advantages and disadvantages to each.

It seems that every time sailors get together in a shoreside pub, the debate over the performance of a Bermuda sailing rig versus the gaff rig comes up. The owner and crew of *Regina-Germania* have avoided the never-

ending question, however, by choosing both, or at least a compromise that includes elements of both.

Built in Hamburg in 1980 and finished at home four years later as a family project, the sturdy 14-metre vessel has been cruising the Baltic and the North Seas since. Designed to be flexible, the rigging can be modified by the crew of six to match the predicted wind conditions. When this schooner races across the open Atlantic as part of Rendez-Vous 2017, she will encounter a variety of wind conditions quite different than her usual fare along the coasts near home. For this voyage, the crew have prepared for anything and can set different sails to suit. The current choice of a wishbone gaff rig was determined by the expected prevailing winds and the likelihood of having to face stiff headwinds or following breezes.

The idea of the wishbone (or fishbone) spar attached to the top of the mainsail is that the masts can support the wishbone while it holds a wider four-cornered sail, catching more of the upper breezes than would a triangular sail. Setting the sail and wishbone is quicker than raising the heavy gaff spar, and a lot fewer blocks and tackles are needed. The angle of the mainsail can be changed with a minimum effort to suit the wind direction, and the schooner is steered accordingly.

This adaptation of a wishbone spar has not put an end to the debate, but it does offer sailors something else to try to catch the wind, and after all, sailing a tall ship is all about making the fine adjustments that might add even the slightest bit of added speed. What could be more important than that?

Rona 11

HAMBLE, ENGLAND

Built: 1991
Class: D
Rig: Bermuda-rigged ketch
Length: 21 metres
Hull: Fibreglass
Owner: London Sailing Project
Crew: 23
Website: www.ronasailingproject.org.uk

Photo: Sail Training
International

Starting from Royal Greenwich, which is very close to her home port, Rona 11 will bring significant open ocean experience to the race to Portugal, Bermuda, and through to Boston. By Canada Day, she will be dockside in Charlottetown before sailing on to Miramichi and Quebec City for the huge Parade of Sail there and then returning to Halifax for the race to Le Havre.

The Rona Trust is also known as the London Sailing Project. It operates four sail training vessels in Great Britain; their first one, *Rona*, was acquired

Photo: Simon Paquin (ÉcoMaris)

back in the 1960s. The name for that ketch came from the legend of a Maori woman who cursed the moon for not shining one dark night. The moon-goddess heard her complaint but instead of coming out from behind the clouds, she lifted the Maori woman up to the moon to forever be the face we see from earth.

Carrying the name onto the newest vessel in the London Sailing Project's fleet is *Rona II*, a Bermuda-rigged ketch built in 1991. Her crew of twenty-three operates mostly between England and France, but the opportunity to visit North American ports, including an Atlantic crossing, is the type of special challenge the Rona Trust was designed for.

Ordinarily, their training adventures are one day to a week long, focusing on youth and adults who can benefit from the training experience. On board, new crew members quickly learn to step out of their comfort zone and to adopt a team spirit. In fact, they are rarely given a choice; sails need to be set and constantly trimmed, navigation must be learned, and meals must be cooked.

Once back on land, their new sense of resourcefulness and teamwork gives them an awareness and self-confidence adaptable to future challenges. At least, it has worked so far for the over twenty thousand sail trainees in Rona Trust's fifty years of going to sea.

Roter Sand

RIMOUSKI, QUEBEC

Built: 1999
Class: B
Rig: Gaff-rigged ketch
Length: 20 metres
Hull: Steel
Owner: ÉcoMaris
Crew: 18
Website: www.ecomaris.org/expeditions-saint-laurent

In her role as Quebec's sailing environmentalist, Roter Sand *will journey down the St. Lawrence to northern New Brunswick and be a part of Caraquet's Canada Day festival. Retracing her route, she will join all the other vessels in her home province for Canada's 150th birthday celebrations and Rendez-Vous 2017 in Quebec City.*

Prior to coming to Canada just three years ago, *Roter Sand* had spent fifteen years as a floating leadership school on the Elbe River in northern Germany. Even when she was being built, students had full input into the carpentry, welding, engineering, and mechanics that created this gaff-rigged ketch.

A story is told that the sail training vessel was named after the red sands near the lonely lighthouse that stood at the mouth of the Elbe for one hundred years. The lighthouse, of the same name, was being fully restored as a get-away-from-it-all hotel at the time the gaff ketch was being built.

Photo: Sailonboard.com

Purchased and brought over to Canada by ÉcoMaris, a non-profit organization located in Rimouski, Quebec, she is one of the few tall ships based in that province and the only environment-oriented training vessel. French is the working language on board, and the province's flag flies proudly from her mast.

Designed to be a shallow-draft vessel, *Roter Sand* has the manoeuvrability needed on the St. Lawrence River, especially in the small ports along the Gaspé coast and the Baie de Chaleur.

All the topics central to sail training are taught on board. Four professional sailors lead up to fourteen trainees or sea cadets through navigation, knots, rigging, weather forecasting, and ship maintenance. The focus is as much upon where she sails, however, as how she is sailed. The river's ecosystems and marine species receive specific emphasis. Students could have no better access to the ecology of the river, its threats, assets, and its marine mammal populations, than from the decks of *Roter Sand*.

St. Lawrence II

KINGSTON, ONTARIO

Built: 1953
Class: A
Rig: Brigantine
Length: 16 metres
Hull: Wood
Owner: Brigantine Inc.
Crew: 28
Website: www.brigantine.ca

Being headquartered in Kingston, so close to the festivities in Quebec City, St. Lawrence II *will rendezvous with the other tall ships there for the festival. Then she has a busy month, sailing down to St. Peter's, Lunenburg, Digby, and Annapolis Royal in Nova Scotia, plus Saint John and then along the eastern seaboard of the United States.*

Perhaps the first vessel anywhere to be expressly built for young sail trainees, certainly the first in Canada, this brigantine slipped down the ways from her shipyard in Kingston, Ontario, in 1953 and into the hands of Royal Canadian Sea Cadet Corps St. Lawrence. With the rest of the ship finished by local craftsmen, as well as those sea cadets and talented volunteers, *St. Lawrence II* was so successful that two more sail training vessels were commissioned for the Toronto area.

Brigantines like this one became popular almost two hundred years ago because they are quick and manoeuvre more easily than a sloop or schooner. In historical times, that made them popular with pirates and privateers. With the foremast square rigged and the mainmast fore-and-aft rigged without any square sails, these craft used to be called schooner brigs.

The program continues to offer youth the focused training it is known for and *St. Lawrence II* is still crewed mainly by cadets, but the program has broadened its focus to include any participants under the age of eighteen. Indeed, the captain and executive officer are usually the only crew members over that age. Other than those two senior officers, all the leadership roles aboard are filled by senior trainees, who act as petty officers. They pass along the knowledge that they themselves acquired on previous trips, reinforcing the learning and sharing it at the same time. The balance of the twenty-eight- person complement thereby receives a type of peer-to-peer training which is unique in the sail training fleet. Like *Lord Nelson* and other sail training vessels, crewing aboard *St. Lawrence II* for longer trips qualifies young sailors for the Duke of Edinburgh Gold Preliminary, Practice, and Qualifying Journey stage, not to mention offering the thrill of sailing into New York City, where she is scheduled to travel later in 2017.

Sorca

MAHONE BAY, NOVA SCOTIA

Built: 1978
Class: B
Rig: Schooner
Length: 13 metres
Hull: Wood
Owner: Think Sail Inc.
Crew: 8–9
Website: sailtraining.ca/portfolio-item/think-sail-sorca

From her home port of Mahone Bay, Sorca will sail to Bermuda to meet the flotilla and join their race back to Boston. Her mission then is to sail to Caraquet, joining two other yachts and the fully rigged Nadezhda for the Canada Day festivities and continue up the St. Lawrence to Quebec City for the official Rendez-Vous 2017 Parade of Sail.

Skimming over the waters of Mahone Bay is what *Sorca* was designed for, but she can also face the ocean gales, having first crossed the Atlantic during the tall ships race in 1984 and visited Bermuda and the Caribbean numerous times since.

Photo: Think-Sail Inc.

The agile schooner was built in 1978 by famed Lunenburg wooden boat builder Murray Stevens and baptized with the Gaelic word for the brightness she reflects.

The original choice of rigging made *Sorca* a Bermuda schooner. Sometimes called a Marconi because of the stablizing connections of her two masts, it is said to resemble the antenna used by Guglielmo Marconi when he successfully sent the first transatlantic radio signals from Glace Bay, Nova Scotia, in 1902.

All schooners have the fixed connection between the two masts, but having this right at the top precludes the use of a triangular topsail set high

Photo: Sail Training International

in the gap between the masts. That would be where extra racing sails could be set and some skippers complain that without them, it is more difficult to compensate for a loss in speed when sailing off the wind.

The upside is a vessel with fewer ropes and perhaps a faster hull speed in upwind conditions. The alternative to the Marconi rig, with fore-and-aft, triangular mainsails, is the gaff sail. This is how the familiar *Bluenose II* is rigged, with that term stemming from the stiff gaff or spar that secures the top side of the foresail and the mainsail. It is raised with multiple ropes and tackles.

There is also some space at the top of the masts on gaff-rigged schooners for adding triangular topsails. When schooners were the working boats of choice on the fishing grounds, that was not often done unless the conditions were favourable and the crew was trying to squeeze every bit of hull speed out of the wind.

The design of tall ship rigging, particularly in a race, can place significant strain on both the masts and the sails. When cotton was the only fabric available, it was important to make sure that as the sails were raised and the wind filled the canvas the tensions on all corners of the sail were evenly applied. Large four-sided gaff sails were often damaged by the uneven winds aloft, particularly when adjustment of the gaff was needed to change the vessel's direction.

Naval architects would therefore choose the Marconi rig for their schooners, sacrificing some speed but saving the sailcloth. Today, synthetic materials give sails much more strength and durability, and the traditional wooden masts are being replaced by stronger composite materials. Racing skippers are taking advantage of these new technologies and are now returning to gaff rigging in some cases. Even *Sorca* has decided to remain flexible and can raise either rig.

Spaniel

RIGA, LATVIA

Built: 1979
Class: C
Rig: Bermuda-rigged sloop
Length: 17 metres

Hull: Fibreglass
Owner: Private owner/operator
Crew: 12
Website: www.lbma.lv

Spaniel *will race from Portugal to Bermuda to Boston and then share the Hector Quay with four other visiting tall ships as Pictou celebrates Canada Day. The sloop will be a part of Rendez-Vous 2017 in Quebec City and then return to Nova Scotia and the Halifax waterfront to prepare for the race back to Le Havre.*

Spaniel likes the wind. Her small crew of six, plus six young trainees from Riga, Latvia, has entered almost every tall ship race in northern Europe since she was acquired in 1998 and has won its fair share of awards.

Photo: Stuart Birnie/
courtesy of bermudasloop.org

Each of the new trainees is encouraged to become part of the larger team, preparing the vessel in the spring, participating in weekday training voyages, and studying the theory of sailing. Of course, having fun together is a big part of their program as well, following the adage that the more games you play on land, the more races you win at sea.

Originally designed as a single-handed ocean racer and built in Poland in 1979, *Spaniel* is a very fast sloop. When the wind is brisk, she can do over fourteen knots. Working together as a team at that speed, though, takes on a new meaning when everybody has a job to do and very limited space to do it in.

Competing with other vessels as a Class C tall ship, *Spaniel* has a Bermuda sloop rig that is very efficient at responding to changes in the wind. Where heavier boats might slow to a stop when the winds disappear at night, *Spaniel*'s crew trims the sails continually to catch even the slightest change in the breezes.

Running with stiff winds and catching the slightest of zephyrs will be important skills for the young team members during both crossings of the open North Atlantic for Rendez-Vous 2017.

Spirit of Bermuda

HAMILTON, BERMUDA

Built: 2006
Class: C
Rig: Bermuda-rigged schooner
Length: 28 metres
Hull: Wood
Owner: Bermuda Sloop Foundation
Crew: 8
Website: www.bermudasloop.org

With so many sailors from all over the world arriving on their shores and favourable breezes for most of the year, it is no wonder that Bermudians decided to build their own sail training vessel.

Spirit of Bermuda has the classic schooner-rig design that made the island's fishing fleet famous for two centuries. Her three tall masts stretch thirty metres above the sea, making her almost uncatchable when sailing into the wind. It is that thrill of ocean racing that captivates the students in Bermuda's middle schools and has them lining up for a tour of duty on board.

The permanent crew of eight on Spirit welcomes fifteen to twenty-four sail trainees when she is preparing for ocean trips. On board the schooner, youth of all social and ethnic backgrounds are introduced to character and educational opportunities only available from hands-on learning.

Crew accommodations are not luxurious but hot showers and air conditioning are available, which are unheard of on many tall ships. The youthful crew is still expected to step out of their safe zone, though,

*Photo: Karen Ryan/
Sail Training International*

work through each difficult task, and encourage their crew mates to do the same. Trainees completing their voyage remember the relationships made on board and the cultural exchanges, however, rather than the hard work and close quarters of their floating classroom.

After a winter of racing among the Caribbean islands, *Spirit of Bermuda* will cover the seven hundred nautical miles to Halifax for the huge tall ship regatta planned for the first of August. Her visit to Nova Scotia will continue over the next two weekends in Louisbourg and Lunenburg, before heading back south to her home port of Hamilton.

Spirit of South Carolina

CHARLESTON, SOUTH CAROLINA, US

Built: 2007
Class: B
Rig: Gaff-rigged schooner
Length: 29 metres
Hull: Wood
Owner: South Carolina Maritime Foundation
Crew: 30
Website: www.spiritofsc.org

Spirit of South Carolina will join the ocean race from Bermuda to Boston, then participate in Canada's 150th birthday celebrations on the Port Hawkesbury waterfront. After joining the many other tall ships of the Rendez-Vous 2017 flotilla in Quebec City, she'll travel back down the river to Louisbourg and Halifax. The festival in Shelburne will attract four tall ships in August, including Spirit of South Carolina, *then it's on to the sailpast in Annapolis Royal and a weekend of dockside entertainment in Saint John.*

Spirit of South Carolina is a gaff schooner, like several others in the Rendez-Vous 2017 flotilla. This American build, however, is much newer and longer, and she carries larger sails. When seen from the Ravenel Bridge over the Cooper River in Charleston, her silhouette is unmistakable.

With all six sails set, including the topmost fisherman staysail, she is as impressive as any sailing vessel ever to visit the historic harbour.

She was launched in Charleston just ten years ago to honour that city's all-but-forgotten maritime heritage. Her professional crew of nine offers charter cruises around the harbour approaches and through the winding channels of the wide Cooper River. Designed with the classic lines of the original pilot schooners so common in the early days of Charleston and carrying a lot of sail, she is an elegant symbol of the state's nautical past.

When visiting communities up and down the Atlantic seaboard, *Spirit of South Carolina* can accommodate twenty-one sail trainees. They are introduced to an experiential learning curriculum designed as a hands-on opportunity to see the seas around them.

She also introduces host communities to American sailing ships, something she did in Havana this past winter as the first American registered vessel to enter that port in many years.

Tree of Life

NEWPORT, RHODE ISLAND, US

Built: 1991
Class: C
Rig: Gaff-rigged schooner
Length: 22 metres
Hull: Wood/epoxy/fibreglass
Owner: Private owner operator
Crew: 6
Website: schoonertreeoflife.com

Like the Spirit of South Carolina *and* When and If, Tree of Life *will participate in Canada's 150th birthday celebrations and the Festival of the Strait on the Port Hawkesbury waterfront and be back in Halifax for the Parade of Sail there.*

Another wooden schooner, with the added touches of a fine yacht, this vessel has been cruising the eastern seaboard of the US since 1991. *Tree of Life* is registered in Newport, Rhode Island, but was actually built by Covey

Island Boatworks in Nova Scotia, following the lines of a classic Baltic trading schooner.

Over 22 metres long and finely crafted of strengthened fir and spruce, the ship has hatch covers and bright work of mahogany, maple, and teak. The many other touches combine old-world traditions with modern convenience. She has three staterooms and features a ship's library and

Photo: Brian Commette/
NorthropandJohnson.com

office with additional accommodation. Her main salon is a relaxed space with a dining area and TV lounge. That and the well-appointed galley make her a favourite for sail training, charter cruising, and blue ocean voyages.

Since she started to take on trainees, several hundred have learned maritime history, navigation, and the preparation of fine cuisine at sea. She has already sailed around the world twice with her owners, a crew of four, and two sail trainees. That kind of experience tends to test a vessel and its crew, but the experience has been so rewarding they have no intention of retiring. *Tree of Life* is for sale, however, for $1.25 million US. As any owner of a tall ship can attest, nobody owns one forever; they just take care of them for a while.

Unión

Built: 2015
Class: A
Rig: Four-masted barque
Length: 90 metres
Hull: Steel
Owner: Peruvian Navy
Crew: 257
Website: www.marina.mil.pe

The newest member of the Sail Training International flotilla, BAP Unión is still on her initial shakedown cruises. Next year, she will join the eight other fully rigged ships from South America and sail from Brazil to Cape Horn, then north to the Panama Canal and finish in the Mexican port of Veracruz after more than four months of sailing.

The Peruvian Navy only took possession of their fully rigged barque *Unión* in January of 2016. A long time in the planning, the beautiful four-masted barque was purpose-built to expand the training available to the country's midshipmen and cadets.

BAP *Unión* was christened in honour of an historic naval corvette involved in sea battles with Chile in the 1880s. This namesake, one of

Photo: Elelch /
commons.wikimedia.org

the largest tall ships in the world at 90 metres in length, will be dedicated
not to warfare but to sail training. As a registered sea school, and with a
total complement of 257 men and women, she can deploy her twenty-six
sails to take her into peaceful waters around the world. The ship's interior
includes an auditorium, a library, computer labs, and classrooms to
instruct new recruits in celestial navigation, meteorology, oceanography,
and hydrography. The navy also recognizes the potential to use the vessel

for scientific research, emergency relief in case of natural disasters, and humanitarian aid.

The ship's mission is more than sail training, however, as symbolized by its figurehead. The bronze sculpture is a representation of an ancient Incan emperor raising an arm to Inti, the Sun God. The crew aboard BAP *Unión* is very proud of its Incan heritage and shares examples of the many unique facets of Peruvian culture when in foreign ports.

Vahine

HELSINKI, FINLAND

Built: 1972
Class: D
Rig: Bermuda-rigged ketch
Length: 20 metres
Hull: Fibreglass
Owner: Sail Training Association of Finland
Crew: 12
Website: www.staf.fi

Vahine will race from Portugal to Bermuda to Boston and then spend Canada Day in the birthplace of Confederation, Charlottetown. The sleek white ketch will then sail up the St. Lawrence to be a part of the Rendez-Vous 2017 flotilla in Quebec City and back down to Halifax for the traditional sailpast and prepare for the return race to Le Havre.

A ketch by any other name would be just as pretty. *Vahine*, which is a Tahitian word for woman, is indeed an attractive ketch.

Built in 1972 by legendary Nautor's Swan, a shipyard located in a part of Finland where the sea is frozen solid for five months of the year, she was designed to offer all the joys of cruising combined with the opportunity for racing success. A sister ship to *Vahine* actually did win the Whitbread Round the World Race in 1973-74, but this ketch is not just a racing platform.

What is even more appreciated by her crew is how well she handles in rough seas.

She wasn't designed specifically for ocean racing. In fact, she was built a little too heavy to take good advantage of the lighter winds, but put her into heavy going, and she seems to lift her nose like a thoroughbred.

Sail Training Association of Finland, the organization that leads that country's sail training program has been active with a number of vessels since 1983 and requires no previous sailing experience on any of them. Young or old, the trainees aren't taught to sail as much as they learn by sailing. STAF emphasizes team work and taking responsibility, asserting that the basics of seafaring come along through participation in setting the sails, navigating, rigging, and stepping out of one's comfort zone.

Recently, the organization was pleased to announce that since their beginning they have accommodated almost twenty-one thousand trainees,

Photo: sailwhenandif.com

from twelve years of age to adults. That has included crossing the Atlantic sixty times and having to sail into all the heavy going that entailed.

They are even more proud of the emphasis placed on a new environmental campaign called Sails for Environment. Similar to the Blue Flag Scheme that *Fair Jeanne* and other Canadian vessels are a part of, it shows that the sail training vessel is pledged to protect the seas she sails on. The personal interest for sailors on *Vahine* is the Baltic Sea, which they feel is suffering greater pressure than most bodies of water because of the heavy industrialization around it and the restricted tidal exchange of the region.

When and If

KEY WEST, FLORIDA, US

Built: 1939
Class: B
Rig: Gaff-rigged schooner
Length: 19 metres
Hull: Wood
Owner: Private owner/operator
Crew: 12
Website: www.sailwhenandif.com

Coming up from the warm tropical breezes of the Caribbean, When and If *will join one other American vessel in the more temperate climate of Port Hawkesbury for Canada Day celebrations, then sail up the St. Lawrence to be a part of the Rendez-Vous 2017 flotilla in Quebec City. After the huge Parade of Sail there, she'll travel back down the river to Corner Brook and St. Peter's. The Lunenburg Folk Harbour Festival will attract nine tall ships in August, then she is on to Digby and Saint John.*

When a legendary army tank commander commissions a brand-new gaff-rigged schooner, shipyards stand to attention.

So it was with *When and If*, built in Maine for General George Patton who had promised his wife that when and if he got through the war in

Europe, they would sail around the world together. He never did make that trip, but his new boat was so well constructed, fast, and comfortable, that it is still cruising the Atlantic coast of North America.

Built in 1939, she remained in the Patton family for thirty-three years, then was gifted to a sail training school. She was unfortunately badly damaged during a storm in 1994, but because she was so well made, a complete restoration has returned her to a like-new condition.

After another ownership change and relocation to Key West, *When and If* became a regular participant in local regattas and races. Now that visitor restrictions for Americans wishing to visit Cuba have been eased, her sailing plan includes frequent dashes to Veradero. Her captain and the five crew members retain George Patton's dream of sailing around the world with up to six additional sail trainees and insist that both they and their vessel are a long way from being too old to carry it through.

Wylde Swan

MAKKUM, NETHERLANDS

Built: 1920
Class: A
Rig: Topsail schooner
Length: 41 metres
Hull: Steel
Owner: Swan Fan Makkum
Crew: 50
Website: www.wyldeswan.com

With a hundred years of solid Dutch sailing experience, Wylde Swan will race from Royal Greenwich in England to Portugal and Bermuda, then sail up the St. Lawrence to be a part of the Rendez-Vous 2017 flotilla in Quebec City. She'll travel back down the river to Louisbourg in Cape Breton and attend the Lunenburg Folk Harbour Festival. That entertainment-packed weekend will attract nine tall ships in August. Then it's on to Digby, Annapolis Royal, and Saint John before the long sail back to Rotterdam.

Early in the 1900s, herring was the *uber*-abundant fish species in the North and the Baltic Seas. Fleets from all over Europe competed to fill their holds and hurry back to port for the best market price. Fishing boats are made for setting their gear and carrying full loads of fish, not speed.

That meant a new vessel type was needed, one designed to transship the catch at sea and race back to port. The steam trawler *Jeno* was designed for just that purpose. Built in Germany in 1920, she joined a small fleet of market chasers serving that industry for seventy-five years, but with the herring stocks badly overfished and the market failing, *Jeno* was finally retired.

In 2010, Dutch owners bought the hull and transformed it into the largest topsail schooner afloat. She was renamed *Wylde Swan,* and with her speedy hull, fifty-metre tall masts, and oversized sails, her crew hopes to make her the fastest sail trainer in her class.

Style and speed combine to give her a prominent place in the tall ship fleet and have resulted in several trophies for open ocean racing. The quality of her sail training and even her meals are also highly regarded. For work and play, on watch and off, the large main deck is busy with the business of a busy ship. Sailors at work and at play, on watch and off.

However, the thirty-six trainees are accommodated in bunks and hammocks in the main saloon, and that serves to remind them that the life of a sailor is better spent up on deck.

Acknowledgements

Rick Welsford was a constant source of technical detail during the preparation of this book. Jennifer Angel and Kelly Rose, at Nova Scotia's Waterfront Development, as well as Brent Hobson, Halifax Tall Ships liaison officer, offered event information and contacts for the ports, with assistance from:

Wayne Long in Charlottetown
JP Desrossiers and Robbie Rankin in Summerside
Bea MacGregor at Alderney Landing in Dartmouth
Armel Lanteigne and Daniel Landry in Caraquet
Darlene MacDonald in Pictou
Wally Vaters and Lisa Betts in Pugwash
Paula Davis in Port Hawkesbury
Derek Burchill and Lloyd Cameron in Miramichi
Mark Barbour in Sydney, St. Peter's, and Louisbourg
Chris Abbott in Shelburne
Robin Scott and Christa Heyne in Lunenburg
Ben Cleveland in Digby
Jillian MacKinnon in Saint John, and
Andrew Tom, National Defence Headquarters, Ottawa.